"When I first took a glimpse at the Table of Contents for this book my immediate response was "Wow, this is the encyclopaedia of financial advice!" I quickly realized that I was right, and everyone needs to read this (and follow Clayton's sage advice) now! It is vitally important that you educate yourself on financial issues in order to properly prepare for a secure financial future. Clayton will guide you on a journey of discovery. Discovering what it takes to really be rich; in the purest sense of the word. I will tell you, however, that the absolute best way to get the most out of Your Money Puzzle is to review the entire book, front to back, AND follow through on the exercises. True value is what you'll find on the pages within this book"

Peggy McColl, *New York Times* Bestselling Author http://www.destinies.com

"Clayton Moore's Your Money Puzzle is both inspiring and practical. He offers specific techniques to attract financial security into your life. His life-altering insights will help you change your personal energy around financial issues and guide you toward the financial stability you desire."

Sandra Anne Taylor, *New York Times* Bestselling Author of
Quantum Success

"If you want to be financially secure (and who doesn't?) Clayton Moore has written a book that is practical, inspiring and purposeful. If you work with the ideas presented in 'Your Money Puzzle' you will create the financial security in life that you really desire. The pieces of the money puzzle are laid out perfectly for you to discover your true potential to take control over your own financial destiny. This remarkable book is sure to change a lot of lives, including yours."

Gerry Robert – Best Selling Author of several books including *Conquering Life's Obstacles, The Magic of Real Estate and The Tale of Two Website: A Conversation About Boosting Sales On The Internet, The Millionaire Mindset: How Ordinary People Can Create Extraordinary Income*, www.gerryrobert.com

"Clayton Moore has created a phenomenal work that will help you create the financial security you have always desired. His practical and inspiring insights together with a masterful plan to create whatever you want from life will set you on the path to greater abundance in all areas of your life."

David Riklan, Founder – SelfGrowth.com

"An extremely comprehensive and informative guide to financial mindset and psychology - highly recommended."

Marcus de Maria. Wealth mentor and trading coach,

www.investment-mastery.com

"Before reading Your Money Puzzle, I understood very little about personal finances and retirement planning. I now have a realistic, actionable plan for creating financial security – and it's far easier than I thought!"

Danielle Dorman, working mother of two

YOUR MONEY PUZZLE

YOUR MONEY PUZZLE

PIECING TOGETHER YOUR FINANCIAL SECURITY

CLAYTON J. MOORE

ISBN: 978-0-9561916-1-8

Contents

One And Only You

Every single blade of grass,
And every flake of snow—
Is just a wee bit different …
There's no two alike, you know.

From something small, like grains of sand
To each gigantic star
All were made with *this* in mind:
To be just what they are!

How foolish then, to imitate—
How useless to pretend!
Since each of us comes from a *Mind*
Whose ideas never end.

There'll only be just *one* of *me*
To show what I can do—
And you should likewise feel very proud,
There's only *one* of *you*.

That is where it all starts—
With you, a wonderful,
unlimited human being.

James T. Moore

FOREWORD

PEGGY MCCOLL,
NEW YORK TIMES BEST SELLING AUTHOR

It was Bob Proctor who said: "There is so much good we can do with money. Without it, we are bound and shackled and our choices become limited."

Would you like your choices to be limited? I'm certain you don't, or you wouldn't have made the investment in Clayton Moore's book Your Money Puzzle. When I first took a glimpse at the Table of Contents for this book my immediate response was "Wow, this is the encyclopaedia of financial advice!" I quickly realized that I was right, and everyone needs to read this (and follow Clayton's sage advice) now!

There are many people who will tell you that money isn't important or money doesn't make you happy or money won't solve all of your problems, but I will tell you that without it, as Bob Proctor said: our choices become limited. Being ignorant (in a state of not-knowing) is not a blissful state. It is vitally important that you educate yourself on financial issues in order to properly prepare for a secure financial future.

Mae West (along with a number of other folks) was known to have said: *"I've been rich and I've been poor. Believe me, rich is better."* Regardless of who said it, this quote has a lot of truth in it.

What do you choose for yourself? What type of financial future would you like to experience? Is it your desire to be financially comfortable? Read on and Clayton will guide you on a journey of discovery. Discovering what it takes to really be rich; in the purest sense of the word.

Your Money Puzzle has been designed in a way to read from the beginning of the book, in a logical format, all the way through to the end of the book. You will realize that this is not only a fabulous book, it is also a workbook, and Clayton has cleverly created exercises for you to follow in order for you to experience the maximum result. Another great benefit of Your Money Puzzle is that you can simply go to different sections of the book and invest focused time studying the sections that most appeal to you. I will tell you, however, that the absolute best way to get the most out of Your Money Puzzle is to review the entire book, front to back, AND follow through on the exercises.

True value is what you'll find on the pages within this book. Here's a glimpse of some of the gold nuggets of wisdom you will discover:

How Following the Crowd is a Dangerous Plan
How to Build Your Own Assets to Give You The Income You Desire
The Multiplier That Accelerates Your Wealth
How to Create Your Money Mountain
How Much is Enough?
Decide to Design Your Life Instead of Making a Living
Create Your Own Equity
The Biggest Risk – Doing Nothing at All!
...and so much more!

The best investment you will ever make is an investment in yourself. I encourage you to invest the time to discover, understand and apply Clayton's principles, and I'm convinced, within a relatively short period of time you will begin to reap the benefits.

Your Money Puzzle is not just a book – this is a workbook or guidebook for you to create an abundant life.

—Peggy McColl, www.destinies.com

CONGRATULATIONS

CONGRATULATIONS on making an excellent investment in your financial future. Over the course of reading this book and completing the exercises included in each chapter you will be taking your life to an all new level. Once you have learned how to piece together your money puzzle, you will experience extraordinary results and unparalleled personal fulfilment in your life.

But wait! Before you start on this journey it is very important that you think very clearly about what it is that *you* personally want to gain from investing the time and money in learning how to piece together your financial security. So, I would recommend that you take a few minutes of your time now and answer the following three questions:

1. What is the single biggest reason why you have invested in *Your Money Puzzle—Piecing Together Your Financial Security*?
2. What is the one specific area that you want to learn the most about from studying this book?
3. What must happen for you in order to make this learning experience wildly successful?

I would love to hear from you with your answers to these questions, as this will help me to help and support you further on your path to financial security. Please feel free to e-mail me with your answers. You can reach me at:

yourmoneypuzzle@claytonjmoore.com

Good luck! I look forward to hearing about the results you achieve as well as the people you have the privilege to impact in your life based on what you've learned.

Warmest Regards,

Clayton J. Moore

INTRODUCTION

"Life is difficult."

THESE were the words that M. Scott Peck chose to begin his fantastic book *The Road Less Travelled* back in 1978, and I believe that they are still as true today as they were back then. When it comes to planning our financial futures, life is as difficult now, if not more difficult, than ever before—and this is the reason that I have written this book for you.

Many authors open their books by sharing their story. Although you can read about me in the About the Author section of the book, there are two important reasons why I have decided not to share all the details of my personal and professional history: Firstly, you don't really care about me or my story. Secondly, what you do care about is *you*. You care about your family, your problems, your concerns, your safety, your comfort, your money, and your life. If you are worried or concerned about your financial future—particularly in light of the changing economic climate—know that you are not alone. The financial world has changed drastically over the past few decades, and as a result, millions of people are now realizing that their long-held dreams of an easy retirement and living comfortably once they finish working is very unlikely to come true.

The purpose of this book is to:

1. Raise your awareness about the threats and trends that are going to affect your immediate and long-term financial health
2. Provide insight into your thinking process so you can deliberately manage your thoughts to create a better life
3. Support you in clearly assessing your current financial reality so you can determine where you are and where you are headed
4. Teach you how to earn more money and—even more importantly— how to keep more of what you already earn
5. Show you that *time* is your biggest asset and help you gain *power* over it

6. Help you to clarify exactly what you want, so you can live your life on your own terms and achieve anything that you desire

7. Help you understand what is holding you back and preventing you from achieving what you want

8. Demonstrate how risk is an essential prerequisite for creating a more financially lucrative future

9. Share innovative strategies that you can act on immediately to build *financial security* and *independence*

10. Help you understand the power of *leverage* and how to use it to make money

11. Allow you to see how the quality of the decisions you make right now will affect your future

Finally, and perhaps most importantly, this book has been written with the aim of helping you realize the potential that you have to become truly wealthy in every area of your life.

To get the most out of this book you will need to participate as much as you possibly can. It's not enough to just read passively and then set the book aside, hoping that things will somehow get better in your life without taking action. There is no "one plan-fits-all strategy" for helping you create more financial abundance. This is your life and nobody else's, and you are the one who needs to be actively involved in creating it as you want it to be.

By reading this book, answering the questions, and completing the exercises at the end of each chapter, you will begin to see clearly where your life is, in relation to where you want it to be. If you use the book actively and participate fully, I promise that your financial life will improve dramatically, and in very short time, you will be well on your way to financial independence.

M. Scott Peck went on to say in his book *The Road Less Travelled*:

"This is a great truth—one of the greatest truths. It is a great truth, because once we truly see this truth, we transcend it. Once we truly know that life is difficult—once we truly understand and accept it—then life is no longer difficult. Because once it is accepted, the fact that life is difficult no longer matters. Most do not fully see this truth that life is difficult. Instead they moan more or less incessantly, noisily or subtly, about the enormity of their problems, their burdens, and their difficulties as if life were generally easy, as if life *should* be easy."

The financial world is constantly changing, and you need to be aware of what these changes are and how they are going to affect you. Getting stuck with what has happened in the past is one of the biggest dangers you face. By taking an honest assessment of the difficulties and problems you will need to overcome in order to become financially successful, you will gain the awareness to blaze a more rewarding path. Let's begin!

NEVER PLAN THE FUTURE BY THE PAST

Kathleen Casey-Kirschling was reportedly the first baby born in 1946, and as a result, she is known as the first person to usher in the "Baby Boomer" generation. "Baby Boomer" is the term given to the 100 million plus births that exploded in the western world in the ten year period following the second World War. This generation of people, who have been setting world trends since 1946, will likely continue to have a massive influence on our economy for many generations to come.

And as most baby boomers well remember, there was a time when all you had to do was go to school, get good grades, find a safe, secure job with a pension scheme, and be a loyal employee, and you could reasonably expect to retire and live out your days in a comfortable manner with a few luxuries thrown in now and again. For the past few generations the majority of workers could expect to live reasonably well in retirement on the financial benefits they had been promised.

Times have changed. In today's world, most people lack the basic financial education to understand what is happening with their own finances, let alone to understand what is happening in the world's economy. Going to school, getting good grades, and finding a safe secure job with a pension scheme is just not enough anymore. Nowadays, in fact, long term job security doesn't come anywhere close to ensuring long term financial security.

The majority of people are also unaware that over the last two decades the responsibility for our financial well-being has been shifting. The responsibility for our financial future no longer rests in the hands of the government or the company we work for; it is entirely up to us as individuals. Our future depends on our ability to invest wisely now and to effectively plan ahead. Only by becoming completely accountable for ourselves can we know with reasonable certainty that we will build up enough money to survive on when we eventually finish work and retire.

Our economy is currently undergoing the most dramatic change that we've seen in sixty years—and I am here to tell you that this is not a phase or a trend but an entirely new way of life. Take a deep breath, because in this "new economy," your pensions, investments, retirement, and income are all at risk.

The "New Economy" is being shaped in part by Kathleen Casey-Kirschling and the other 100 million or more Baby Boomers who will soon retire. The institutions we have relied upon in the past are completely unprepared for what lies ahead. There are gaping holes in social and economic provisions—and this was even before the effects of the momentous changes that we have seen as a result of the recent credit crunch that brought about the demise of many of centuries-old financial institutions.

A full-scale crisis is looming, and anyone who is planning to rely on the government, state, or a private pension to guarantee a comfortable retirement is in for a rude awakening. There are, in fact, nine threats and trends that may be putting your financial security at risk, and it's essential that you understand what these are:

THREAT 1: AN AGEING POPULATION

We are living in a rapidly ageing society.

The number of U.S. citizens over the age of sixty-five is rapidly increasing while the number of those age sixteen and under is shrinking. In fact, there are more than 36 million Americans over the age of sixty-five today, and this number is predicted to grow to over 70 million within twenty-five years. Right now in the U.S. alone, 4.6 adults turn sixty-five every minute, and this is predicted to rise to 8 adults turning sixty-five every minute by 2025!

For the first time in history the number of British people who are over the age of sixty-five exceeds the number of those who are under sixteen. Over the next thirty years the percentage of those age sixty-five and older is expected to rise from 16 percent to 25 percent of the population! This is part of a global trend: life expectancy is increasing while birth rates are stabilizing or declining across most developed nations.

Our ageing population is threatening the welfare state because major welfare systems such as pensions, health, and long-term care are organized on a "pay-as-you-go" basis, meaning that the current adult working population finances the needs of older people. As the number of older people grows in relation to the working population, we will begin to see this financial arrangement unravel. The old-age dependency ratio—meaning the number of people age fifteen to sixty-four relative to the number of people over age 65—is decreasing, so as older people draw pensions, more demand will be placed on governments, companies, and pension fund resources.

You may be wondering, in light of all this, who is going to pick up the bill for your retirement? There was a time when the government could be expected to shoulder the costs of the elderly; however, this too is rapidly changing.

THREAT 2: THE DECLINING VALUE OF GOVERNMENT PROVISION

Social Security in the U.S. was once seen as a "floor of protection" for Americans. However, since 1979, Social Security's contribution to retirees' income relative to their previous wage earnings has been steadily declining. Without intervention, Social Security is expected to go into the red in 2013 and be totally broke by 2041, with an estimated shortfall of $15 trillion. The retirement benefits of Social Security are dependent on both the number of working people that are paying taxes compared to the number of retired people, and the willingness of these working people to be taxed at ever higher levels to meet the shortfalls.

The value of the state pension in the U.K. has been radically scaled back by the abolishment of the link between state pensions and earnings. Before 1980, the basic state pension was increased annually in line with average earnings, or wages. But, since 1980 the basic state pension has instead been increased in line with inflation. The measurement of inflation can be more easily adjusted than wages, and so this has had a devaluing effect on the real value of the basic state pension!

Because earnings tend to rise faster than inflation, the effect has been dramatic. In 1980 the basic state pension was over 20percent of the value of average earnings. By the year 2000 this percentage had reduced to less than 15percent. Projections are that by the year 2030 it will be under 10percent and by 2050 will account for less than 7percent of an individual's average earnings. Therefore there are major concerns about the risk to people who are under-saving. Unless major changes are made to the degree of responsibility we take for generating our own resources in retirement, we will suffer serious pension shortfalls and a big reduction in our standard of living.

THREAT 3: INFLATION INCREASING IN A SLOWER ECONOMY

To combat our credit problems, governments and central banks around the world have been cutting interest rates and pumping cash into the system in order to try and achieve a soft landing. While this may seem like a good short-term solution, it creates a long-term problem: more money in the system could mean higher prices and a devaluing of the money that is in circulation. This in turn may keep an already slowing economy from growing, and for the first time since the 1970s there is a growing risk of "stagflation," a combination of stagnation in the economy and inflation. This may well result in lower wages, fewer jobs, and more layoffs, which are all increasing concerns for families.

Inflation is calculated using a cross-section of costs reflecting the spending patterns of the average person. Several factors can cause the national inflation rate to differ from your own experience of prices. One major factor is how you spend your money. If you spend more than the average person on housing and transport, and prices for these goods and services rise sharply, then your "individual inflation rate" would be higher than the average.

Another factor that influences how inflation affects you individually is the level of income you have to begin with. If you are on a low and relatively fixed income, then you are going to be affected much more by inflation than if you are on a higher income that is increasing faster than the inflation rate. Age Concern in the U.K. has called for more help for pensioners, as new research from the Institute of Fiscal Studies suggests it is pensioners that are being hit harder by inflation than anyone else.

Inflation is shaping up to be a serious threat to financial markets, to the economy as a whole, and to us as individuals. From housing and food to transport and shipping costs, inflation is really squeezing the value out of our money.

THREAT 4: JOB SECURITY AT AN ALL-TIME LOW

These are just some of the headlines we saw in the media in 2008 alone:

United States	United Kingdom
Unemployment, Job Losses Both Worse than Forecast	Bleak Prospects for U.K. Job Market
Disappointing Job Reports	EMI Confirms Thousands of Job Losses
Manufacturing Job Losses Keep Climbing	Job Market Losing Its Shine As Slowdown Deepens
More States Losing Jobs	Slowing Eurozone Job Market Sends a Warning
Planned layoffs Increased for Third Month in a Row	U.K. Job Losses Likely Permanent
CEO—Minimum Wage Ratio Soars	Planned Layoffs Increased For Third Month in A Row
Job Losses worst in Five years	Manufacturing Jobs Situation Has Worsened
Huge Job Losses Set off Recession Alarms	Gloomy Outlook for U.K. Job Market
Americans Have Bleak View of Job Market	Government Statistics Mask Tough Job Market
Jobless Rate at Fourteen Year High after October Losses	Damaging Cuts in Overtime Set Off Alarms
U.S. Job Losses Soar	Jobless Rise Highest In Seventeen Years

With headlines like these, it's easy to see that the old security blanket of a job for life and a nice pension at the end is a very unrealistic goal in today's economy. The fact is, most people do not work for only one employer for forty years anymore, and if moving jobs and changing careers is the new status quo, then it's up to us to look for a better solution for investing in our future financial security.

THREAT 5: THE SAVINGS GAP

Americans are seriously under-saving for their retirements, and current estimates show that 45percent of Americans age fifty-one to sixty-one do not have enough assets to support 90percent or more of their current living expenses. Less than 40percent of workers even have a pension—guaranteed or not—and among those who do have a pension, the average worker qualifies for only about one-third of their pay when they are due to retire.

For the first time in modern history, the personal savings rate in the U.S. has fallen into negative territory with 63percent of Americans acknowledging they don't save enough and 36percent saying they spend more than they can afford. Current estimates show that 46percent of the U.K. workforce is not contributing to a pension scheme and that up to 7 million British people are seriously under-saving for their retirements.

In the U.K., the official Government pension policy has been steadily shifting towards "voluntarism." This means that the state wants you—not them—to take responsibility for your pension. The government has pledged to invert the 60/40 split between state and private pensions in pensioner incomes, which means that the state will increasingly provide only a limited safety net, and the onus is placed squarely on you, the individual, to provide for your own financial security in retirement.

What's even more troubling is that the majority of people simply do not realize that it is now up to them to create their own financial security, and this is creating a massive savings gap in the provisions for many millions of people.

So if, despite the fact that the responsibility is being passed on to us to provide for our own financial security later in life, we are still not contributing to our own futures, then we must ask ourselves this question:

Who will look after us when the time comes for us to retire?

THREAT 6: LIFE EXPECTANCY

Human beings are living longer than ever before. Life expectancy is now at its highest level ever, and all evidence suggests that this trend is only going to continue its upward climb in the future.

Children born in the U.S. can expect to live a long life, with males living an average of 75.2 years and females an average of 80.4 years. Life expectancy for Americans once they have reached the age of 65 has also reached its highest level with men living to an average age of 82.2 years and women living to an average 85.0 years.

In addition, because people are now expected to be active for longer into retirement, they will need to generate the resources to fund these activities. As Christian Weller, senior economist at the Center for American Progress stated, "People are having to work longer. If this continues, the average American will not have enough to retire on and will not be able to retire."

Similar findings can also be seen in the U.K. According to the Office for National Statistics in 2007, the average life expectancy for men is now at 76.9 years, and for women it is at 81.3 years. Also, life expectancy once you reach the age of 65 has now increased to 81.9 years for men and 84.7 years for women.

So, on average we are now living seventeen to twenty years past the age of 65, traditionally the normal age of retirement. The fastest growing segment of the 65+ age group are the men and women reaching the age 85, and currently about 2percent of the population is age 85 and older; that's over a million people in Britain alone, and this number is predicted to double in the next twenty years and triple in the next thirty years!

These longevity facts highlight how important it is to carefully plan for the future, as we need our income to last for a lot longer in retirement than the generations that have gone before us. The cost implications of this increasing longevity are arrestingly bleak. Peter Hain, a Member of Parliament in the U.K., while in his role as Secretary of State for Work and Pensions, noted that, "Unless we act now, we will bequeath a nightmare both for future pensioners, plunged into poverty, and for future taxpayers grappling with the consequences."

THREAT 7: LIVING LONGER IN POOR HEALTH

Living longer in good health is a blessing. However, living longer in poor health may not be. In fact, a report by Prudential Group in November 2008 revealed that nearly 20percent of people stop working because they are not well enough to continue.

With the control of typhoid, cholera, polio, measles, and other infectious diseases, life expectancy has increased substantially over the last century. However, this longevity is marred by a rise in chronic disease with its associated costs.

Chronic diseases such as heart disease, cancer, and diabetes are now the leading causes of disability and death, and about 30percent of adults have some form of chronic disease. (Source: Improving Chronic Disease Management, Dept of Health 2007).

In anticipating the cost of healthcare, we must take our ageing population into consideration, for the prevalence of hypertension, heart disease, diabetes, and other chronic diseases increase with age. It has been reported that 82percent of people over age sixty-five have at least one chronic condition.

In order to meet the changing demands for healthcare in an ageing population, Spending on Medicare in the U.S. and the NHS in the U.K. has risen substantially. Medicare spending in 2008 is projected to be $442 billion, and by 2016 this is expected to rise to $861 billion. That's nearly a 50percent increase in just eight years. Similarly in the U.K., in 2003 the NHS budget was £65 billion and by 2008 it was £106 billion. That is almost a 65percent increase in five years! What increase will be needed in the next ten years and beyond, and who will pay for it?

THREAT 8: THE UNCERTAIN VALUE OF PERSONAL PENSIONS

Younger pensioners are relying more than ever before on funds from private pensions, and this reliance will continue to grow as the government and companies struggle to meet the costs of looking after an ever-increasing pool of ageing retirees.

However, the majority of pension schemes are linked to the stock market, and stock market volatility has a big impact on the value of the funds. The facts are that pension deficits are growing, and surpluses are shrinking.

In addition, over the last ten years, U.S. retirement assets have shifted considerably away from employer sponsored defined benefit pension plans. In 1997, 56percent of retirement assets were in defined benefit schemes and 47percent of assets were in defined contribution schemes, such as 401(k)s and Individual Retirement Accounts (IRAs). By 2017 this split is expected to be 10percent to 90 percent in favor of defined contribution schemes.

At the close of 2007, 79percent of defined benefit pension schemes in the U.K. were in deficit, and this is a worsening trend. Because of falling investment returns, payouts from private policies have dropped more than 50percent in the past ten years, while at the same time, the annual income from the reduced funds has dropped by 40 percent!

When it comes to final salary or defined benefit pension schemes, a major shift is also underway. In January 2008, a poll conducted by the National Association of Pension Funds, part of the Pension Advisory Service, predicted that in the future the vast majority of employers will offer defined contribution schemes, or money purchase schemes, instead. Many companies are closing down defined benefit scheme, and within a decade very few defined benefit schemes are likely to be left in the private sector. As the pool of retired former employees increases year by year, it seems, these pensions are just too expensive and risky for companies to provide.

THREAT 9: WORKING LONGER INTO GOLDEN YEARS

If you think you will have saved enough money when the time comes to retire, you may be fooling yourself. The fact remains that today's retirees are facing a longer retirement with nest eggs half the size of those fortunate to have retired a decade ago. In addition, the growing pension crisis means that many people will have to work for much longer into their retirement years just to survive. Even now, it has been reported that 69percent of Americans will rely on working at least part-time in retirement to cover basic expenses and receive employer health benefits. Also, more than 1.2 million U.K. pensioners have taken menial jobs, for which many of them are over qualified, in order to support themselves through retirement.

The average age of retirement is already rising, and with the increase in life expectancy, millions of people simply cannot afford what could well turn out to be a thirty year retirement.

And this is before Kathleen Casey-Kirschling and the 100 million plus other baby boomers start hitting retirement age.

WILL FUTURE GENERATIONS BE ABLE TO RETIRE?

It should be evident by now that we as individuals must provide for our own security in retirement, and that retirement for the next few generations to come will be extremely challenging.

When the Baby Boomer generation retires it is going to put a huge strain on the resources of our governments and welfare systems; longer life expectancy will require each individual to have accumulated a much larger nest egg at retirement—all the while the lack of incentives and financial means limit our ability to save more.

The message is clear: We have got to change the way we plan for our futures.

Our financial environment has changed radically, but our financial education and habits have not. Many people are coming to the conclusion that they simply don't know what they need to know to secure their futures.

The traditional middle class approach to investing for the future has been to save as much money as you can in your pension, then buy a house and watch its value increase over time. These methods of financial planning are no longer a reliable means for getting rich or creating a nest egg to retire on—in part because these strategies were never designed to create wealth; they were designed to create security.

However, as we have already seen, this misconception of creating security could very well turn out to be a *false* sense of security.

Both the U.S. and U.K. governments have only mentioned two options for creating a better retirement: Save More or Work Longer.

Unfortunately, there are two major problems with these two strategies:

1. Why would anyone in their right mind save more of their hard-earned cash into investments that are just not working in the first place?
2. Why would anyone want to keep working long into their golden years just to make ends meet?

Options no one has mentioned—but that this book will cover are:

- Creating multiple sources of income
- Getting higher returns on the money you invest
- Building wealth-creating assets

Wealth-creating assets are those that provide investors with higher-than-market returns, allow investors to minimize their risk, and allow them to optimize their energy, efforts, and money.

The cycle of creating cash to buy assets, which creates more cash to buy more assets, is the strategy of the wealthy. By taking the time to educate yourself about your options for the future, and by gaining financial knowledge you are actually reducing your risk.

Robert Kiyosaki, in his book *Cashflow Quadrant*, observes:

"Education is more important today than ever before. But we need to teach people to think a little further than just looking for a secure job and expecting the company or the government to look after them once their working days are through. That is an 'Industrial Age' idea, and we aren't there anymore. The rules have changed."

MONEY PUZZLE MASTERY EXERCISES—
THE THREATS AND TRENDS FOR YOUR
FINANCIAL FUTURE

After reading this introduction and seriously thinking about its content, what three things are most important for you to remember about *the threats and trends for your financial future?*

1. _____
2. _____
3. _____

How has learning this affected the way you think about your financial future?

_____
_____
_____
_____

What actions do you intend to take from what you have learned in order to create a more successful and abundant future?

1. _____

2. _____

3. _____

4. _____

5. _____

RETIREMENT AND PENSIONS

DO YOU KNOW WHAT RETIREMENT REALLY IS?

BY educating yourself about retirement you will gain the knowledge to break free from the trap of working just for the money, and can start living life on your own terms, doing what you want, when you want, and with whom you want.

Freedom comes from understanding your options—yet the majority of people do not really understand what their financial future holds in store, because they have never taken the time to really learn about what is going to happen when they finish work.

Very few of us approach learning as a life-long process. For most, in fact, education stops after college. Some of us choose professions that require additional training, but courses designed to educate us about ourselves, our money, and our financial future are virtually non-existent.

If you—like many—are not actively involved in understanding your finances and planning your future, now is the time to set yourself on the path. As Eric Hoffer explained in his book, *Reflections on the Human Condition*:

> "The central task of education is to implant a will and a facility for learning; it should produce not learned but learning people. The truly human society is a learning society, where grandparents, parents, and children are students together. In a time of drastic change it is the learners who inherit the future. The learned usually find themselves equipped to live in a world that no longer exists."

Retirement is a major milestone in life. If we want to stop working one day, so we can enjoy our time doing things we want to do rather than toiling away at jobs just to pay the bills, we must take the time now to prepare ourselves for retirement. However, retirement continues to be the one subject that most people do not really educate themselves on and this could prove a very costly mistake in our modern world.

The real definition of "educate" is to "educe from within." This meaning is very significant in today's world, as it is falling more and more on us as individuals to take responsibility for our own financial security. We all need to "educe from within" the knowledge, confidence and capability to become financially independent enough to support ourselves in retirement.

This book will teach you the keys of becoming financially independent. Once you know how to earn money, keep money, and control money, you will be able to generate a lifetime of income to fuel your dreams and desires.

TIMES HAVE CHANGED

The economic climate we are living in today is dramatically different from the one that existed even a generation ago, yet many of us have failed to update the way we plan for our eventual retirement. In the old economy, people used to finish school, go to work for one employer for forty years, and then retire to enjoy a few years of rest before departing this earth.

In the old economy, if you didn't have a company that looked after you in retirement, then the government would take care of you. Companies and governments could afford to look after you then, because they had cleverly worked out that if you were to finish work at the age of sixty-five, then they wouldn't have to pay you for long, because the average life expectancy was not much greater. As a result, most people have adopted a very passive attitude about retirement, relying on someone else to look after them when their working years wind down.

However, as we have moved from the industrial age to the information age, companies and governments alike simply cannot afford to pay people in retirement as they once did, so it is falling more and more on individuals to provide for themselves. Relying on someone else could prove fatal to our comfort and security later in life.

A NEW PARADIGM OF RETIREMENT

The word paradigm comes from the Greek "paradeigma" and means, "model, pattern, or example." While many definitions of the word have been offered over the years, my own definition of a paradigm is this:

"A paradigm is a set of rules, beliefs, and habits of thought about a topic that is wildly held as true."

Let's look at the current paradigm surrounding retirement.

It is still such a widely held belief by the majority of people that someone else should look after us in retirement, be it the company we work for or the government.

The change in paradigm to taking personal ownership of your own retirement is critical to retirement planning, because it will put you in complete control over your own destiny, and you will have no need to rely on anyone else to look after you later in life. The sooner we realize that it is our 100percent responsibility to look after ourselves in retirement, the sooner we can begin asking ourselves some very important questions. For example:

- Why am I doing what I'm doing with my money?
- What could I do better with my money to ensure that I am building for a more secure and lucrative retirement?

By freeing ourselves from the paradigm of thinking that others will look after us, we can then start to design our own lives, plan when we want to finish work (not when someone says we can finish), and decide how much we earn when we finish work (not what someone says we can have).

WHY RETIRE AT AGE SIXTY-FIVE ANYWAY?

One of the biggest paradigms to establish itself in society over the last one hundred or so years has been the determination that sixty-five is the most optimal age to retire.

This rule was originally established by a very clever German Chancellor who wanted people's votes, and so introduced the notion of looking after people with a state pension at the age of sixty-five. This was massively popular with the voters and was the beginning of state pension schemes around the world. What no one realized is that because this clever man had already calculated that the average life expectancy was only sixty-two at the time, he knew that he would never have to pay out on his promise to half of the people!

Because this precedent was set, most other developed countries established similar state pension schemes, and companies soon followed suit, introducing pension schemes to take effect at around age sixty-five. As it turned out, this also became an effective strategy for companies in the industrial world to get rid of older, less physically able workers and replace them with younger, stronger people who were likely to be more productive.

Another thing to consider is that retirement creates a radical change in a person's lifestyle. While you may have more free time to enjoy life, the older you are when you retire, the less likely you are to have the health or the energy to enjoy this free time.

So, why not aim at becoming financially independent in life at a far younger age, so that you can enjoy the benefits of having the free time *and* the energy to do everything you have always dreamed of doing?

ROUGH SEAS AHEAD

A very real and formidable financial challenge lies ahead that will likely affect not only our generation, but future generations as well. Within this century alone, pensions have gone from being a source of financial salvation to a massive source of worry and confusion. As we have already explored, one of the main causes of this change is the fact that we are now living longer, and our longevity is expected to increase further as medical advancements are made. Although this increase in longevity has many advantages, it also creates a huge strain on both the government and private companies, traditionally the main providers of people's pensions.

As the number of people over the age of sixty-five grows in relation to the number of people who are still working, government resources will become increasingly strained. The only foreseeable option to meet the shortfall is an increase in taxation on the reduced working population in order to fund the growing retired population.

The resources of private companies are also being stretched as more and more people want to retire and draw their pensions from funds that are not being contributed to by enough current workers. Realizing that they can no longer afford to use shrinking funds and resources to guarantee the pensions of a growing number of people, many companies are switching to defined contribution plans rather than the more traditional final salary schemes.

Defined contribution schemes, also known as money purchase schemes, place no responsibility whatsoever on the employer to pay a person's pension in retirement. What comes back to the individual will be dependent on fund performance and what that money will buy for you when you get to retirement – rather than being based on an worker's final salary. Therefore all of the risk is being passed onto us as individuals and away from the companies for whom we work.

In 2010, the baby boomer generation is due to start hitting the age of sixty-five. This global population of 100 million or more people has been of working age since the early- to mid-1960's, the period when stock market pension schemes (pooled investment funds) first became popular. These schemes are where most of companies' pension funds are invested, and therefore, over the last forty years or so, there has been a massive amount of money going into these funds month after month. When money goes into something it tends to increase in value, and this has resulted in stock markets rising substantially over the last forty years.

What will happen, however, as more and more of these 100 million plus baby boomers start taking money out of their pensions as they retire? Well, no one can predict fully, but in the same way that money going in pushes value up, money coming out could well cause these stock market investments to fall. The impact of reducing fund sizes will likely mean that the number people will get back in retirement could leave them with a severe financial shortfall for the rest of their lives.

WHY ISN'T THE GOVERNMENT TELLING US WHAT WE SHOULD KNOW?

In the same way governments have ignored the bankrupt Medicare and NHS systems, they have also ignored the growing problem with pensions, cost of living increases, and rising debt. Why? Because the majority of government officials are more concerned with remaining in office than in really solving these issues.

They may try to win votes by promising lower taxes, but the reality is, to eradicate the pension crisis and the Medicare and NHS funding shortages, governments will need to implement large scale tax increases—and this is news that no one wants to hear.

Given the nature of this Catch 22 situation, many governments have opted to simply ignore the issue. While steps have been taken to educate the public that planning for retirement is the responsibility of each individual, many people still don't realize what this means, nor do they understand the options that are available to help them. It's quite possible that another reason that governments have not acted sufficiently on the pensions crisis is because they really do not know what other options to introduce for people.

In his book, *Prophecy*, Robert Kiyosaki explains this problem well, stating:

> "Governments solve many problems for the good of society. It is the government that uses our taxes to provide military defence, fight fires, provide police protection, build roads, provide schools, and provide welfare for the needy. But there are problems that government cannot solve, and when those problems are pushed forward they often become bigger and bigger problems. This problem of financial survival once a person's working years are over is a monster of a problem that is growing bigger and bigger, because too many people expect the government to solve what is really a personal financial problem."

FAILING TO PLAN = PLANNING TO FAIL

During their working years, most people are so caught up with family commitments and maintaining their current lifestyle that they do not properly plan for their retirement until it is too late. In fact, the majority of people don't give much thought at all as to what retirement really is, when they want to retire, or how much income they will need to secure their futures. Most people actually spend more time each year planning their holiday or Christmas than they do designing their lives and planning their futures.

There is the famous quote by Alan Lakein, the well-known expert on personal time management that states, "Failing to plan is planning to fail." This basically means that by not planning a prosperous and financially stable retirement, you are unwittingly planning for a bleak, financially unstable one.

Everyone is going to retire one day, so why not retire on *your* terms and not according to someone else's plan? You can, if you choose to, start planning what your retirement is going to look like and how much you will need in retirement, so that when that day comes, you will have all the resources you need. The earlier you start planning your retirement the easier it is to build up the money that you will need to provide the life you want to live.

Let's say you want to retire at the age of fifty, and to do this, you determine that you'll need to generate an annual income of 25k. In order to build the fund that is necessary to provide this income, you will need to invest. If you leave it until the age of forty to start investing the money necessary to provide you with the 25k per year, meeting this goal will be a great uphill struggle, and quite possibly impossible to achieve. However, if you started planning at the age of twenty, you then gain an additional twenty years to build the resources you will need, and the chances of you retiring at the age you want and on the income you want will be infinitely more likely.

By not planning for your retirement you also run the risk of other financial commitments taking greater priority over the disposable income you have. Before long you may find it a lot more difficult to set aside what you need in order to create the life you want.

WHAT DOES RETIREMENT MEAN TO YOU?

What does retirement mean to you really? Have you ever given much thought to it?

Most people toil away in their jobs—jobs they drifted into without much thought, because they needed to pay the bills—with the hope that one day they will finish working, put their feet up, and enjoy a few years of relaxation.

Have you noticed, however, that most wealthy people continue to work way beyond the normal retirement age? And have you ever wondered—as I have—why this is so often the case?

I have come to understand that because wealthy people solved the money puzzle early on in life, they work not for a pay check, but because they enjoy the work they are doing.

Now, just think. If you had enough income coming in so that you did not have to go to your job would you still get up and go to work in the morning? Probably not!

Retirement is just about replacing your income as soon in life as is possible, so that you are free to do the work that you love. Why work all of your life just to retire and enjoy a few years, when you can become financially free and independent, and retire to a long and healthy life of doing the things that you enjoy most?

The whole notion of retirement as a final reprieve from work at age sixty-five is actually flawed for a number of reasons.

First of all it, assumes that you dislike the work you have chosen to do throughout the most mentally and physically capable years of your life. This is a farcical explanation, as why would you work for thirty or forty years at something you dislike, just so that you can retire at the end of it?

Secondly, the majority of people who do retire in the traditional way retire on far less income than they were earning while working. This retirement income now has to last for thirty-plus years, which means your reduced income will be eroded year after year by inflation, and your standard of living throughout retirement will drop dramatically through what should be your golden years.

Thirdly, if you are one of the very lucky minority who does get to retirement on a glorious pension, then it means that you are probably a very ambitious, hard working person with very high goals and aims in life. If this is your situation, I predict that within weeks of your retirement you'll be bored out of your mind and will soon be off to start another business or new job.

Therefore, why wait until you get to sixty-five to retire?

The sooner you solve your own money puzzle, the sooner you'll free yourself to live your life on your terms from this day forward.

The fact is, even in today's difficult financial climate, there are limitless options for you to replace your earned income with passive income, but each of these paths must start with some basic steps:

- You need to change your thinking about retirement, money, and time, and then assess where you currently are in life.
- You need to set a goal for your standard of living, and determine what income you'll need to create to provide lifestyle you desire.
- You need to plan your path to financial freedom and follow that plan until you succeed.

Real power is having the ability to choose how to live your life. By understanding what retirement really is, you open up unlimited ways to move forward intelligently and create financial independence far earlier in life than the traditional forms of pension planning can ever do.

HOW MUCH IS ENOUGH?

One of the things that I believe prevents people from becoming financially independent and retiring young and rich is that most people have no idea exactly how much money they will need in order to provide them with the lifestyle they want.

A practical definition of financial independence is having enough money set aside to maintain your desired standard of living without having to go to work for it. The goal of retirement is to place yourself in a position where you no longer have to work to pay your bills, and can therefore do what you want with your days and live your life with much more choice than if you are constrained by a lack of money.

Most people think that they could survive on less income in retirement, and that may be true for some. But, if you actually think about when you spend most of your disposable income, you'll probably realize that you spend it in your time off work. Once you retire, your time off increases massively, so it's safe to assume that you would probably need *more* money to occupy the increased time you have available.

By investing just a little time working out what you would actually need to retire from your job, you may be surprised at just how easy it is to create exactly what you want!

WHAT IS OUR HEALTH COSTING US?

The health of the nation has an indirect but critical influence on our retirement planning. As we have already discussed, medical advancements are increasing longevity, which puts additional strain on the resources of government, companies, and personal pensions.

At the same time, the overall health of the nation is getting worse, with obesity at an all time high, and diabetes and heart disease continually increasing. With chronic diseases such as these on the rise, welfare systems like Medicare and the NHS are shouldering much of the burden. This situation is likely to get worse with time, creating an even bigger strain on governments—and eventually tax payers.

TRADITIONAL ADVICE IS LEAVING US SHORT

More than ever, traditional financial planning is leaving people without the knowledge and the tools to effectively build the funds they will need to retire. This is due in part to the fact that the advice given by most financial planners is limited, because it's restricted to the plans available to them and the rules surrounding those particular pension contributions.

In fact, because the majority of financial advisers are either working for insurance companies or banks, their main objective is actually not to help you plan your retirement on the whole, but to sell you one of these company's products. And, because they earn commissions based on sales performance, you have to question whether the advice they are giving you is intended to ensure a secure retirement at the end of your working career or to ensure that they take home a nice pay check at the end of the month. Most financial planners have targets set for them by their employers as to how many pensions they have to sell, and they may therefore recommend a pension in order to hit a sales quota, rather than to provide you with the most appropriate vehicle for your retirement fund.

Once people set up pensions, they can easily develop a false confidence and put the matter of retirement out of their minds—yet when questioned about the details of the pension they established, very few actually understand what the benefits are going to be.

If they had just studied it in greater depth, they would have realized that the cost of saving for their real needs in retirement may not have been accurately represented by these so-called financial advisers.

Let's look at some examples:

Let's take a 30 year old U.S. citizen who is earning $30,000 per year in today's economy. Let's assume he or she wants to retire at the age of 65 earning the same $30,000 per year (in today's terms). Let's assume also that this person expects to live for 30 years in retirement. Assuming a 5% annual return on their money, this person would need to set aside $1,890,789 by the age of 65. To accumulate this amount in their pension fund would require an annual contribution of $20,000 per year. They are only earning $30,000 per year before taxes to begin with and in order to retire at age 65 earning the same level of income they need to pay in $20,000 every single year over the next 35 years! Is this affordable? I think not!!

(Source: www.americanfunds.com/retirement/calculator)

Next, let's take a UK citizen who is 30 years old and is earning £30,000 per year. Let's assume he or she wants to retire at 65 earning the same £30,000 per year. If this person saved £100 per month into a pension for the next 35 years the amount that he or she would get back to live on would be only £3172 per year. To generate the intended £30,000 per year, this person would actually need to save £939 per month into their pension for the next 35 years! Is that affordable to most people earning £30,000 per year? I think not!!

(Source: www.pensioncalculator.org).

And yet, strategies such as these are advised by many financial planners.

You may wonder why these professionals do not advise their clients to buy property, start a business, or create multiple sources of income as part of their retirement planning. The answer, plain and simple, is that nobody pays them to dispense this type of advice.

WHAT EXACTLY IS A PENSION?

The problem with pension planning is that most of us put off learning what a pension really is, and this leaves us insufficient time to plan ahead for a wonderful retirement.

Understanding what a pension really is will inspire you to take responsibility for your future financial well-being because it will give you the knowledge and facts about what you need to plan for your future.

If only we realized what a pension really was when we start out working, then more and more of us would stand a better chance of retiring from "work" at a much younger age, and could then devote our time to things that we really *want* to do and not just "work" to pay the bills.

It's only with accurate thought into what a pension really is that we will realize the truth: we can all achieve a wealthy retirement while we are still in the prime of our lives. Accurate thought means separating the facts from mere information. It also means separating the facts into the useful and the useless. So, if we look at pensions and retirement we need to really look at all the "information" that comes out of the traditional routes of pension planning, and look at the bare facts as to how this is going to affect us later in life. We also need to discern which of these facts is most useful in helping us to us achieve our goal of becoming financially independent.

So, what is a pension?

The Cambridge dictionary defines a pension as

"a sum of money paid regularly by the Government or a private company to a person who does not work anymore because they are too old or they have become ill."

Dictionary.com defines a pension as

"a fixed amount, other than wages, paid at regular intervals to a person or to the person's surviving dependents in consideration of past services, age, merit, poverty, injury or loss sustained."

No wonder the majority of people give no thought to planning their retirement! Thinking of a pension as something that is paid to us by the government or private company when we become too old or ill to provide for ourselves is not a very inspiring view of retirement at all! The time has definitely come for us to redefine what a pension means to us as individuals; and *this* is where things get very exciting.

My definition of a pension is

"an income that comes to us on a regular basis from capital built up or income generated by us without having to go to work for it—i.e., passive income."

In this definition we do not need to rely on the government, or any organization, for that matter. A pension, as I am defining it, is created by building up sufficient capital to generate passive revenue sources that will provide us a regular income for the rest of our lives.

When a pension is defined in these terms, then, it's easy to see that our only limitations are those that we impose upon ourselves. We are the ones who get to decide how much capital and passive income we want to build up in order to provide the income we desire.

TYPES OF PENSIONS

Understanding the different types of pensions that are available to you and how they work will enable you to realize that your own future financial security is truly in your own hands, and you cannot rely on anyone else to provide your income once you finish work.

In both the U.S. and the U.K. there are basic benefits available from the government when you retire. Now, everyone who still thinks relying on the government to provide us with enough income to achieve anywhere near a decent standard of living is really taking some massive risks with their financial futures. However, as we saw earlier, huge portions of the U.S. and U.K. populations are not contributing to a pension, so relying on the government to provide income later in life is a very real risk that many millions of people are currently taking.

The next type of pension that may be available to you is a company pension from your employer. These can be arranged in one of two ways:

The first is a Final Salary or Defined Benefit scheme. With this type of pension scheme the pension that is paid to you is based upon your final earnings with the company and entitles you to a fraction of this final salary for every year that you worked for the company. The company directs a percentage of your monthly salary into the company's pension fund, which then pays out income to all the former employees who have since retired from the company. As we discussed earlier, this places a huge burden on the company, and with average life expectancy rates rising each year, it's not surprising that most companies no longer offer final salary schemes to new employees and have reverted to the more common type of company pension scheme: a Money Purchase or Defined Contribution plan.

With this type of scheme, the only thing that is defined is the amount of money that goes into the plan. What gets paid out is based solely upon the fund's investment performance. These types of schemes are stock market- based pooled investment funds where your money goes into a pot with all of the other investors and is then invested in the stock market by fund managers in order to provide the growth on your money.

The only control you have over this type of scheme is the money that you pay out every month into the scheme. You have no control at all, other than maybe choosing what funds to invest in, over how the money is invested or on what type of return you make, and so you are left completely at the mercy of others as to what you will get back at the end of the day when you want to draw your pension.

The third type of pension scheme is called a personal pension scheme, IRA or self directed retirement fund. This works exactly the same way as a Money Purchase scheme, the only difference being that you pay directly into a stock market investment fund rather than making the payment through your company.

These traditional investment vehicles simply don't provide a decent enough return on your investment, and what's more, the people who make the real money on these investments are the companies that are managing the funds. It does not matter whether your scheme falls or rises; they still take their charges out!

It's no wonder that so many working people are not contributing to a pension!

WHAT COULD YOU GET BACK?

Understanding what you'll get back from your current provisions—whether from the state, from your company's scheme, or from pensions that you pay into as an individual—will open your eyes as to the real level of your financial security. It will also reveal a truth that I hope will spur you into action to create your own financial resources for the future. Every type of retirement fund has built-in restrictions that limit your ability to choose when you draw your income in order to retire. Some of these schemes require you to work for far longer than you ever anticipated, as the funds of all schemes are stretched and stretched by our increasingly ageing society because they are required to pay us for a lot longer in retirement than they ever used to.

For example, in 2008, the average Social Security benefit paid to retired U.S. workers was $1086.90 per month (Source: www.ssa.gov), while the basic state pension paid to U.K. citizens in 2008 was £90.70 per week, or £393.03 per month (Source www.thepensionservice.gov.uk).

Could you realistically live on this income and have a good standard of living?

Well, if you are not contributing to any pension, then this is what you are running the risk of living on when you retire!!

Even if you are lucky enough to have a Final Salary company pension plan, and if you are still lucky enough to have one when the time comes for you to retire (who knows what companies may have to do with their final salary pension schemes as they get more and more expensive to the company year after year?), then your best hope is to retire earning two thirds of your final salary at most. You will also be subjected to company's policies regarding when you can retire. I know that in the past a lot of people have been able to retire on a full pension as young as fifty years of age as a result of these final salary schemes. The generation of people who had the opportunity to take part in these schemes were very lucky indeed, as it was before companies really understood the long-term financial impact of paying people a full pension for so many years. If you do want or need to retire early, your income will be penalized very heavily for doing so.

If you have a Money Purchase scheme or a personal pension then you are *really* in the lap of the gods as to when you can retire. In this case, your pension fund is usually used to buy an annuity, which provides you with your pension income—meaning the amount of income you will receive will all depend on the fund's performance.

Annuity rates, which determine the level of income you will receive from the money you have built up in your pension fund, are linked to the number of years your pension will be paid. As the population's life expectancy continues to rise, annuity rates are likely to fall further, meaning a further reduction in the income you will ultimately receive.

The main thing here is that you really need to understand exactly what the pension provisions you currently have in place are going to give you, and when. Only with accurate knowledge will you be able to make the informed decisions that will build the financial stability you need and want in your retirement.

YOUR MONEY IS LOCKED AWAY FROM YOU

Because your money is tied up and locked away from you in your pension scheme, *when* you can retire and *how much* money you will receive when you do retire is left totally to the discretion of someone else and not you. If you are in a company pension scheme, then you cannot retire until your company says you can. With our ever ageing population, more and more companies will be extending the date they will mandate their employees to work for before they are eligible to retire. Long gone are the days of someone finishing work at age fifty or fifty-five on a full pension, because companies just cannot afford to do this any longer. This alone should inspire you to take a different approach to retirement planning.

If you are in a private pension scheme then, yes, the rules say that in most cases you can take your pension at any age from fifty onwards. But, because you will be drawing your pension for far longer than if you were to retire at sixty-five, then you'll receive far less income.

Whether you are in a company scheme or private scheme, you just cannot access your money whenever you want it. It's locked away until somebody else says that you can receive it. Even then you will not have access to all of your money, as you can only get a small percentage as a lump sum and then the rest as an income for the rest of your life.

YOUR DEPENDANTS COULD BE LEFT SERIOUSLY SHORT

In addition to seriously under-providing for you in retirement, traditional pension plans may also leave your dependents, your spouse, and your children, seriously short in life, should you die.

Most pension schemes offer only a very limited protection for dependents, providing them with just a small percentage of what you were receiving while you were alive.

If you do decide that you want to protect your fund a little more and provide more benefits to your dependents, this comes at a cost, and your pension will be reduced substantially for this benefit.

On the other hand, if you were to build your own asset fund, then, should you die, any income paid to you could be passed directly to your dependents, and none of your money would be lost. Obviously inheritance tax issues could arise, but with careful tax planning this can easily be avoided.

WHY DO THE WEALTHY THINK DIFFERENTLY ABOUT PENSIONS?

The wealthy don't see retirement as a time to slow down, stop working, and live a meagre life with a lower income than they were accustomed to before they finished work. As a result, they think of pensions in a completely different light than do the majority of people.

Most often, the wealthy are not just working for the money, but because they love what they do. Because they solved the money puzzle early enough in life, they are now able to focus on doing what they love to do, rather than working just to pay the bills.

How many of the truly wealthy people in the world leave their future financial stability to chance by blindly paying into a company pension scheme or a personal pension? Very few, I would guess.

By and large, the rich become rich not by going to work and saving a little bit of money over time in a pension scheme. They become rich because they focus on building assets, whether it is property, business, or shares. These assets are the vehicles that have created financial freedom in their lives and have allowed them to pursue whatever they want to in life. They go to work not because they have to but because they love to. So, why would they look ahead to age sixty-five as being a time where they sit back and do nothing for the rest of their lives?

Just think of how many successful people have worked long, long after the normal retirement age of sixty-five. People such as George Burns, Anthony Hopkins, Clint Eastwood, Mother Teresa, Nelson Mandela, Mohammed Al Fayed, and Warren Buffett ... the list could go on.

In today's world of unlimited opportunity, there is nothing to stop any of us from creating enough assets to become financially independent and pursue a line of work that fulfils us for reasons other than making a living. The only thing that will prevent this is not changing the way we think about retirement, pensions, and money—and by not educating ourselves about the different options we have for planning our future financial well-being.

IT'S JUST ABOUT CREATING AN INCOME

The simple truth of the matter is that retirement is all about creating an income that we don't actually have to go to work to earn. The term for this is *passive income.* Planning for retirement is nothing more simple and nothing more complicated than creating an income that pays you whether you are working or not. That's what a pension is. This is a new and more empowering way of defining a pension.

So, if we realize that the sole purpose of a pension is to create a passive income, we can open our eyes and set about creating the income that we want to retire on, and decide when we want this income to come to us.

To begin, you'll need to determine how much money you want to earn when you retire. Most people bury their heads in the sand like an ostrich when it comes to retiring, as they really don't know how much they are going to need to live on when they retire. Once you know how much you'll need, then you can go about creating a plan to achieve it—whether it's investing money in the stock market, buying property, starting or buying a business, or— if you still find this an acceptable strategy—investing in traditional savings routes like pensions.

BUILD YOUR OWN FUND

Building your own fund is the most secure way of planning for your retirement as it puts you in total control over the capital you build up, the income flow you create, and the timing you chose to finish work.

If you really consider all of the limitations and restrictions that are placed on you when you are part of a company or personal pension scheme, you can clearly see that building your own resources is the best way to create long term financial independence.

Creating your own fund will put you in control of your financial destiny rather than at the mercy of others, and allow you to live your life on *your terms* rather than anyone else's.

Building your own fund is all about building real assets that will continue to grow in value and produce an increasing income year after year.

The main asset classes that you can use to build wealth for the future are:

Business
Stocks & Shares
Property

By investing and creating multiple sources of income across all these asset classes, you can multiply your wealth exponentially.

For example, you might be really interested in property as an asset class, but may not have sufficient resources available right now to afford the deposit for the property. However, this problem can be overcome by channelling your skill or passion in a particular area of your life into a business idea that generates a second income. Or, you might have some disposable income that you could put to work in the stock market with the help of some good strategies in this area.

In time, you would then build up enough money to be able to purchase your first property. This property may grow sufficiently in the future that you could then leverage some of the equity to buy more property, expand your business, or build even more money in the stock market.

You may find that your business has grown enough to provide capital for more business growth, more property investment, or more stock market investments. And at other times, your stock market strategies might earn you enough capital to re-invest and accelerate your growth in the stock market, to fund more property growth and further grow your business.

Once you have created the funds that you need to provide you with a regular income without needing to work for it, you can then focus on what it is you really want to do with your life.

We will look a little later at the different asset classes you could invest in to create more wealth in the future, but before we do that you need to understand a number of other key factors that are going to help you achieve all you want from life.

The first step to solving the money puzzle is to awaken to the reality that we are all firmly in charge of our own financial destiny, and building our own financial security is totally our own responsibility.

To break through to a more stable financial future, to create security instead of uncertainty, and success instead of failure, it's imperative that we understand how our minds can be used to control our financial destiny.

MONEY PUZZLE MASTERY EXERCISES—
RETIREMENT AND PENSIONS

After reading this chapter and seriously thinking about its content, what three things are most important for you to remember about *retirement* and *pensions*?

1. _____
2. _____
3. _____

How has learning this affected the way you think about your financial future?

_____
_____
_____
_____

Based on what you have learned in this chapter, what actions do you intend to take in order to create a more successful and abundant future?

1. _____
2. _____
3. _____
4. _____
5. _____

What plans do you currently have for your retirement?

_____

_____

_____

_____

What exactly are your current provisions for retirement going to provide you and when?

_____

_____

_____

_____

What type of pension, if any, do you currently have?

_____

_____

_____

_____

What benefits will this pension provide for you and when?

_____

_____

_____

_____

THINKING YOUR WAY TO A BETTER FUTURE

DO OUR THOUGHTS CONTROL OUR CIRCUMSTANCES?

> *"The action of the mind plants that nucleus, which, allowed to grow undisturbed, will eventually attract itself all the conditions necessary for its manifestation in outward physical form. Now the only action of mind is thought; and it is for this reason that by our thoughts we create corresponding external conditions, because we thereby create the nucleus which attracts to itself its own correspondences in due order until the finished work is manifested on the external plane"*
>
> *—Thomas Troward*

I have been fascinated by the way our thoughts control the events and circumstances of our lives ever since reading the books *As A Man Thinketh* by James Allen and *Think and Grow Rich* by Napoleon Hill. These men wrote their books in the early 1900s illustrating how the power of thought can increase our personal capabilities and results in our lives.

I have subsequently spent several years seeking great teachers of success in life and have discovered that virtually all of them relate our power of thought as a pivotal part of increasing the results we generate in our lives. I have also studied countless theories on the mind and the human brain—the biggest and best supercomputers on earth—to understand how we can better use this fantastic tool in order to create greater financial abundance.

In his book, *The Answer*, author and entrepreneur John Assaraf states that neuroscientists have now estimated that around 98percent of what we know about our brain we have learned within the last ten years or so, and more than 80 percent of what we originally thought we knew has turned out to be false.

We have traditionally been led to believe that our adult brain is hardwired—meaning it's fixed in form and function—so that by the time we reach adulthood, we are pretty much stuck with what we have. We also used to believe that our brain cells were unable to divide and replicate, and that we were born with all the brain cells we were ever going to have—and that once damaged, our brain cells could never be replaced. However, new research has shown that a normal, healthy adult brain can and does actually generate new brain cells and is not nearly as hardwired as we once thought.

In contrast to the old understanding of a hardwired brain, we now realize that the brain changes in response to every new experience, every new thought, and every new thing we learn. This leads to some very important questions:

How many new thoughts have you had lately?

How many new experiences have you had lately?

How many new things have you learned recently?

And, more importantly:

How is your life changing as a result of your new thoughts, experiences, and learning?

> "As a single footstep will not make a path on the earth, so a single thought will not make a pathway in the mind. To make a deep physical path, we walk again and again. To make a deep mental path, we must think over and over the kind of thoughts we wish to dominate our lives"
>
> —Henry David Thoreau

THE BRAIN

Our brain is basically split into two very distinct divisions: our conscious brain and our subconscious brain. Once we learn how these two parts of the brain function together and support each other, we can understand why so many people struggle in pursuit of their goals, and how we can use our brains more effectively to achieve anything we want in our lives.

The conscious brain has also been called our "thinking" brain. However, the term "thinking" could be used quite loosely for the majority of us. It has been estimated that the average human has around 50,000 thoughts a day, however 99percent of these thoughts are exactly the same as the ones we had yesterday!

Earl Nightingale once said, "If most people said what they were thinking they would be speechless." Maybe he was not far from the truth.

> *"Few people think more than two or three times a year; I have made an international reputation for myself by thinking once or twice a week"*
>
> —*George Bernard Shaw*

The brain is basically a switching station for the vibration of thought and the transmission of all the electrical and chemical impulses that rage through our bodies via the five senses; sight, hearing, touch, smell, and taste.

The higher faculties of our mind—memory, wilfulness, imagination, reasoning, intuition, and perception—all reside in our conscious mind and are all used to dream of new possibilities, create ideas, make conscious decisions, assemble plans, carry out intentional courses of action, and regulate behavior.

But, it is our magnificent subconscious that allows us to follow through with the multitude of actions that will be necessary for us to realize our goals.

When we learn something new, as you are going to be doing during the course of this book, we make new neural networks in our brains. Neural networks are individual clusters of neurons that work together and, as Joe Dispenza states in his book *Evolve Your Brain*, "can be used to explain how the brain changes with each new experience, how different memories are formed, how skills develop, how conscious and unconscious actions and behaviors are demonstrated, and even how all forms of sensory information are processed."

We now know that any of us can, at any age, gain new knowledge and formulate new thoughts—and by doing so, we develop new neural networks. This is what learning is.

When we experience something new, sensory pathways in our brains transmit enormous amounts of information about what we are seeing, hearing, feeling, smelling or tasting. Our brains' response is to organize our brain cells into networks of connections that reflect the experience and form a memory.

Therefore, memory is just a process of maintaining the new neural connections that we form via learning. Repetitive thought strengthens these neurological connections, whether they are positive or negative experiences.

So, the old adage of repetition being the mother of all skill is accurate. If we want to learn something new and develop our skills in any area of our lives, then repetition will strengthen our brains neural connections and result in better performance.

The amazing thing is that this repetition does not have to be a physical repetition. We can actually *think* our way to better results!

Tests have shown that people who only visualized lifting a weight with one finger repetitively over a short period of time actually saw their fingers grow stronger, even though they never physically lifted the weight at all. (Source: *Evolve Your Brain* by Joe Dispenza).

Another test was done where one group of people was asked to practice the piano in a structured way, another group was asked to practice randomly with no structure to their learning, and the third group was asked to only visualize playing a structured routine over time. The results showed that the group that mentally visualized playing showed almost the same growth of neural networks as did those who physically practiced in a structured way. The group that played randomly showed very little change in their brains. (Source: pg 48-49 Evolve Your Brain – Joe Dispenza).

Our magnificent brains can process thought, demonstrate intelligence, learn new information, master skills, recall memories, express feelings, create new ideas, and do all of this while maintaining orderly function of all of our bodies' processes.

Our brains are the physical apparatuses through which our minds are produced. The brain is the control center through which the mind organizes all of the metabolic functions that the body require for life and for our survival. Once we understand how our minds function through our brains then we can go beyond the comfort zone of what we already know, and learn the new skills required for building a better future.

When we can get our conscious and subconscious minds working together in harmony, we will be able to modify our whole systems to help us function better in our world and achieve our unlimited potentials.

OUR MAGNIFICENT SUBCONSCIOUS MINDS

To even begin to comprehend a mere fraction of what our subconscious minds achieve every single second of every day—is *staggering*.

The subconscious brain controls all of our body's innate intelligence, involuntary functions, body temperature, blood sugar, pulse rate, heartbeat—even the secretion of the enzymes required to digest our last meal. The millions of processes that are going on inside our bodies each and every second occur with absolutely no conscious effort on our part at all.

The subconscious brain is also where all of our habits—both physical and mental—reside. We walk, drive our car, ride our bikes, tie our shoelaces, speak different languages, and a whole host of other things we have learned in our lives, all without thinking at a conscious level.

Have you ever been driving your car and suddenly realize that you cannot remember the last part of the journey because you were so lost in thought? If you weren't paying attention, then how is it that you didn't crash? It's because your subconscious brain took over, and even though you may have had no conscious recollection of part of the journey, your subconscious got you home safely.

In his book, *The Answer,* John Assaraf, states that one of the greatest discoveries of the past decade of neurological research has been that 96 to 98 percent of all our behaviors are automatic or subconscious. It is in our subconscious where our habits of thought can become so ingrained that our thoughts become our attitudes and beliefs in life.

If we do not update our thinking, we are going to live our whole lives subconsciously, reacting to the events in our lives instead of pro-actively creating our lives the way we would like them to be.

OUR POWERFUL CONSCIOUS MINDS

Our conscious minds allow us to act voluntarily and affords us the free will to make and execute choices concerning what we want to think about, what we want to remember, what skills we want to develop, and what actions we want to take.

We use our conscious minds to exercise voluntary control over our decisions, and to influence our bodies to carry out these choices.

What makes us human is the interaction between our subconscious brains and our conscious brains.

Neocortex

The *neocortex* is the most recent substructure of our brains to evolve and is situated in our conscious brains. It is the part of our brains that really brings to life the fact that our thoughts govern our results and success in life. This part of our brains allows us to modify our actions if we experience negative results, or to repeat our actions if we experience positive results.

The neocortex gives us capacity for rational thought, reasoning, problem solving, our free-willed decision making, planning, organization, verbal communication, language processing, and computation. It gives us the intellect to create new ideas, develop new behaviors, and the skills and to invent new things.

Because of the Neocortex, we can change the course of our lives with one new thought, action, or behavior.

When we are reasoning, planning, intellectualizing, learning, remembering, creating, analyzing, and verbally communicating, then it's our Neocortex that is at work.

The Neocortex is composed of several parts. However the most important structure within the Neocortex is our *frontal lobe*. This is the part of the brain that really helps us to get our conscious and subconscious brains working effectively together in planning and creating better things for our lives.

Our Magnificent Frontal Lobes

When it comes to our thoughts controlling the events and circumstances of our lives, the frontal lobe is where the proverbial rubber hits the road. By regulating the older parts of our brains, the frontal lobe has the ability to navigate our futures, control our behaviors, and dream of new possibilities for our lives. It is the most adaptable to change and can evolve our thoughts and actions for better results in our lives.

Whereas our pre-programmed behaviors, habits, and beliefs are stored in older regions of the brain, the frontal lobe affords us choice, intent, and full awareness, helping us learn from mistakes and shortcomings.

So, everyone who believes that they are stuck with their current circumstances because of their upbringing, education, parents, or past experiences, needs to get a grasp of how powerful their frontal lobes are. They are the seat of our free-will and self-determination, allowing us to choose our thoughts and actions—and therefore control our own destinies.

> *"The greatest discovery of my generation is that human beings can alter their lives by altering their attitude of mind"*
> —William James

The frontal lobe allows us to focus on our desires, generate ideas, make conscious decisions, assemble plans, and carry out intentional courses of action in our lives. It gives us the capability to express any attitude or belief we choose, and to control what we think about our experiences. If we start to make better use of its capabilities, we can truly create anything we want in our lives and realize our unlimited potentials.

The thoughts we think affect the chemical dance that is going on in the brain all of the time. When we take control of our mental state by deliberately choosing our thoughts and attitudes, we can alter the meaning we associate to the experiences we have and results we see in our life.

By using our frontal lobes to capacity, we move from a reaction-oriented way of unconscious living and start intentionally creating our lives the way we really want to live them.

Thanks to the evolution of the frontal lobe, we have the ability to benefit from a focused, intentional, creative, willful, decisive, purposeful mind. If only we would put it to good use!

> *"You've got to develop mental strength. And you develop mental strength with the will. The will is the mental faculty that gives you the ability to hold one idea under the screen of your mind to the exclusion of all outside distractions"*
> —*Bob Proctor*

HOW DOES ALL THIS AFFECT
OUR FINANCIAL FUTURE?

> *"It is the sincere intention that is the essential thing, and this will in time release us from the bondage of habits which at present seem almost insuperable"*
> —*Thomas Troward*

The primary function of the frontal lobe is *intent*. It decides on action, regulates behavior, and is responsible for firm intention. When we are truly purposeful and make conscious intentions to act in a certain way, we activate our frontal lobes. It carries out the intention to focus the attention on one thought, task, or goal, and prevents the mind from wandering to other thoughts and stimuli.

The frontal lobe is the site of our critical thinking—producing our aspirations and desires, allowing us to measure up different situations, analyze current circumstances, and speculate about our options.

Our frontal lobes permit us to learn from experiences and decide what to do differently next time. It devises possibilities, constructs new strategies by forming new thoughts and ideas, and can think out future outcomes.

You will be using your frontal lobe throughout this book to explore new ways of influencing your financial future. By tapping the potential of this part of your brain, you will be able to construct new ideas, thoughts, and actions to increase your future financial security.

As you become clearer about you want, your frontal lobe will keep you focused on living with intent and purpose. As your mind becomes one with this new goal, you will be able to intentionally learn and create new thoughts, feelings, and actions.

It takes effort to contemplate new possibilities for the future, and in order to do so, we have to interrupt the programs that have been hardwired into our brains by our parents, teachers, the media, family, friends, and past experiences. We can only do that when we understand where we are, why we are doing what we are doing, where we want to go, what we really want from our lives, and how we want to live in the future.

We can do this by forming intentions for our lives through accurate thought that will switch on our frontal lobes and propel us into the lives we desire.

We can increase our frontal lobes' ability and effectiveness by asking open-ended, speculative questions that stimulate our higher thinking powers and support us in deliberately creating our futures. Here are some questions that will stimulate your frontal lobe:

- How can I become better?
- What would my life be like if ...?
- What do I really want from my life?
- What do I have to change about myself to achieve my outcome?

As we rise above the familiar routines and patterns of our subconscious minds, we find the inspiration to dream of new possibilities. This is the starting point of creating a better life.

We cannot change the way we think, the way we act, and the way we feel without first altering the possibilities for our lives. The outcome of such changes in thoughts, behaviors, and actions will bring to us new and different circumstances that are equal to what we have set our intentions to become in our lives.

Maybe James Allen was absolutely right, even before understanding any of the information we currently have about how our brains and minds work, when he said back in 1902

"As a man thinketh in his heart, so is he!"

This poem was also written by James Allen in his book *As a Man Thinketh* and sums up how our thoughts can truly make our lives:

"Mind is the Master-power that molds and makes,
And Man is Mind, and evermore he takes
The tool of thought, and shaping what he wills,
Brings forth a thousand joys, a thousand ills:-
He thinks in secret, and it comes to pass:
Environment is but his looking-glass."

As you move through this book, you will learn how to use your conscious faculties to analyze your current circumstances, devise possibilities, and construct new strategies to achieve whatever it is you want from your money, your retirement, and your life.

Rest assured that you can replace the hardwired, conditioned behaviors that your powerful subconscious mind has been using to run your life with up until now. You can replace them with new and better thought out ideas for our world today.

Get involved in creating the life you desire by fully engaging your creative frontal lobe throughout every chapter of this book and setting the intentions that *you* want for *your* life. Do this and I'm sure that you can attain a better, more prosperous financial future.

MONEY PUZZLE MASTERY EXERCISES— THINKING YOUR WAY TO A BETTER FUTURE

After reading this chapter and seriously thinking about its content, what three things are most important for you to remember about *how your thoughts affect your results in life*?

1. _____

2. _____

3. _____

How has learning this affected the way you think about your financial future?

_____

_____

_____

_____

As a result of what you have learned in this chapter, what actions do you intend to take in order to create a more successful and abundant future?

1. _____

2. _____

3. _____

4. _____

5. _____

WHAT DO YOU WANT?

> *"If one advances confidently in the direction of his dreams, and endeavours to live the life which he has imagined, he will meet with a success unexpected in common hours"*
>
> —*Henry David Thoreau*

THE MAGIC OF GOAL SETTING

SETTING goals and having an aim in life is critical to creating a prosperous future, because unless you think deeply about what you want, and decide that you are going to achieve it, all you have in life are wishes that you don't really believe you'll achieve.

Read or listen to the most successful people across all time periods and walks of life, and you will realize that they were all compelled by visions, and set specific goals for the things they wanted to achieve in their lives. In the simplest of terms, they decided what they wanted, and then set about making it happen.

Nobody has ever achieved anything in life without setbacks, hurdles, and obstacles that needed to be overcome. But with a strong enough vision and a big enough purpose for achieving it, anything you want to achieve in life can be achieved. In other words, when the "why" is big enough, you can accomplish any "what."

Deciding and setting a goal to become financially independent as early as you can in life should be everyone's first goal. Once you have created enough income to free yourself from having to live month by month, pay check to pay check, then you are free to live a life totally and purely of your own making. You will no longer be under anyone else's control as to when you can finish work and how much you will make when you do.

If you had already solved your own personal money puzzle, what would you do with your life?

Where would you go?

What would you dare to do that you cannot possibly even think about doing while focused on making a living and trying to make ends meet?

By answering these questions, you begin to build the foundation of your life's vision, from which all worthwhile goals are born.

Most people don't set goals for themselves—not because they don't hold a vision for what is possible in their lives—but because they have never learned how to do it or why to do it.

Creating a vision is one of the most inspiring and important exercises that you can do for yourself. Give yourself the time to sit down and really decide what it is you want out of life, how much money you want, when you want to retire, the places you want to visit, the things you want to have and own, the house you want to live in, the people you want to meet, the relationships you want to have, and the health you want to enjoy. By clarifying your desires and acting on them, you will be well on your way to a prosperous future.

On a practical level, if you don't decide what it is that you want, then how on earth are you ever going to get it?

WORKING TOWARDS YOUR DREAMS

> *"Dream lofty dreams, and as you dream, so shall you become. Your vision is the promise of what you shall one day be; your ideal is the prophecy of what you shall at last unveil"*
>
> —*James Allen*

Most people think success happens once you have achieved or completed something. I believe this mindset is one of the massive causes of frustration and unhappiness in many people.

People become frustrated along the way to their goals because they feel they are not successful while they are on their journeys. They are then frustrated when they get there, because they then realize that the feeling of success of achieving whatever it is they have achieved is a short term experience. Then they are off getting frustrated again while trying to achieve the next thing.

Bob Proctor shared one of the best definitions of success that I have ever come across. He learned it from Earl Nightingale, who arrived at the definition after seventeen years of intensive research:

"Success is the progressive realization of a worthy ideal"

Proctor goes on to describe this definition of success as being in perfect harmony with the laws of the universe and that the four words *progressive, realization, worthy,* and *ideal* on their own have special power and meaning. When brought together, their power is magnified many times and the definition has the potential to transform our lives. If we break these words down we can better understand what he means by them:

> **PROGRESSIVE**—This means we are continually moving in a forward direction, of steady improvement; that there's always a way for things to keep getting better and better
>
> **REALIZATION**—This refers to an intention that is in the process of being realized and coming into materialization
>
> **WORTHY**—This is a reminder to make sure your goals are worthy of you. Do not ask if you are worthy of your goal. Ask instead—Is the goal for which I am trading my life energy—worthy of me?
>
> **IDEAL**—This invites you to set big goals, to visualize the future you want to create in its perfect and ideal state, and to "fall in love" with the idea that you have envisioned.

This definition takes all the frustration out of the pursuit of success because it allows you to feel successful along the way to achieving your worthy ideal. If you are progressively realizing what you want out of life, then this gives you the inspiration to continue doing the things that need to be done in order to achieve your worthy ideal, vision, or goal.

Every day that you move closer to your worthy ideal you can feel successful, and the more successful you feel, the greater the energy you will have to do what it takes to continue.

Most people do not do what it takes to succeed because of three things:

1. They don't have a big enough vision or goal
2. They are not compelled by a big enough purpose or reason why

3. They don't feel successful enough along the way to find the motivation to keep going

When you are actively working toward your life dream and worthy ideals, you will understand the real meaning of fulfilment.

> "An ideal, as such, cannot be formed in the future. It must either be formed here and now or not be formed at all; and it is for this reason that every teacher, who has ever spoken with due knowledge of the subject, has impressed upon his followers the necessity of picturing to themselves the fulfilment of their desires as already accomplished on the spiritual plane, as the indispensable condition of fulfilment in the visible and concrete. When this is properly understood, any anxious thought as to the means to be employed in the accomplishment of our purposes is seen to be quite unnecessary"
>
> —Thomas Troward

THINK ABOUT YOUR FUTURE

Most of our thoughts are habitual and have accumulated over time through our past experiences and cultural conditioning. We go through each day busily trying to fit everything in, but we don't give ourselves time to really think about what we are thinking, nor do we choose the thoughts that we want to think.

When was the last time you really sat down and thought about your future?

What thoughts do you have about the future when it comes to retirement, money, health, family etcetera?

Most people do more or less the same thing every day, every week, every month, and every year, until it gets to the time when they retire on whatever income comes to them from the government and/or their companies. Why? Because they haven't given much thought to their future and are too caught up in thinking about today, their problems, things they have to do and maybe things like their vacations next year, or Christmas. That's about as far into the future that most people's thoughts take them.

However, if they just took the time to sit and really think about the future and what they want out of their lives, their thought processes would start changing from habitual daily thoughts to conscious thoughts about how they are going to provide for themselves and their families in retirement. Instead of being limited by the past, they would start to consider jobs, business, or investments they could employ to realize all their dreams and work towards fulfilled lives.

CREATE A COMPELLING VISION

> *"Dream no small dreams for these have no power to move the hearts of men"*
> —*Johann Wolfgang von Goethe*

Creating a compelling vision for your retirement will inspire you to build a prosperous and fantastic life, both before and after retirement. It will give you a big reason why and a purpose for creating a life of your own choosing and on your own terms.

I believe that too many people accept a vision of their retirement as being one of slowing down, becoming frail and living on less money.

This is hardly a compelling vision, and probably why so many people put off really planning for their retirement.

What if the vision was turned around and retirement occurred at a young age where you had all the time and money in the world to do all the things you have ever dreamed about doing? A vision of not having to go to work just for the pay check at the end of the month but going to work when you want, doing what you want not for the money but for the sheer love and enjoyment of doing it? A vision of taking time off whenever you want; you might travel the world or contribute time and money to great causes. Isn't this a more compelling retirement and one that is worth planning?

If this compelling vision for retirement became your worthy ideal and definite chief aim in life, would it inspire you to take greater action toward becoming financially independent in life and feel successful along the way?

Creating a compelling vision for what you want in your life will also provide you with motivation to keep going through setbacks and challenges that will undoubtedly come along the way.

In his book, *Think and Grow Rich,* Napoleon Hill noted that "persistence is to man that carbon is to steel." Persistence is probably the greatest quality you can ever cultivate when working toward the realization of your vision.

Persistence is much easier when you know *why* you want to achieve something, and this is why creating a compelling vision for your future and for your retirement is *the* most important thing you can ever do.

WE THINK IN PICTURES

We think in pictures.

If you doubt me then just close your eyes, and think of your car, your house, your fridge, your partner, the hotel where you stayed on your last vacation. What did you see?

Did you see a written explanation of these items?

No, you saw a picture of them in your mind's eye.

The pictures that we hold about our futures can either inspire us or destroy our chances of achieving all we want in our lives, because we can paint either good, positive, successful pictures of the future, or bad, negative pictures filled with failure and loss.

If you are very fearful and doubtful about a decision that you need to make for your future, you will paint negative pictures in your mind, such as investments failing, businesses failing, or being laid off from work.

These very same pictures will prevent you from taking the steps you need to take to create the life that you want and will keep you tied like a chain to your current situation.

If you turn those negative pictures into positive pictures about the future, you will paint the picture of investments working out and providing you with financial freedom, of a business that thrives and provides you with limitless income, and of you leaving the job that you hate for one that inspires you and that you love doing.

These pictures will inspire you to take the actions necessary to create the life you want, in spite of the worry and concern that naturally arise when we make bold decisions. You can overcome any worry or fear just by closing your eyes and replacing the negative pictures with positive ones.

IS YOUR LIFESTYLE TODAY AFFECTING YOUR FUTURE?

The lifestyles we choose today have serious affect on our future standards of living because of the effect it has on both our money and our health.

One brilliant quote that I once heard was this:

"We spend the first half of our lives using our health in pursuit of money and the second half using our money to buy our health back."

- Anonymous

Our lifestyles affect our future wealth, because the more of our "today" money that we use on our "today" lifestyles, the less of our "today" money will be available in our futures.

And the less of today's money we devote towards our futures, the lower a standard of living we will create in the future.

Every dollar or pound that we spend feeding our "live for today" lifestyle habits could be redirected to make huge differences in the standards of living we will enjoy in retirement.

The cost of living—even the most basic standard of living —has grown so high these days that most people do not use their money to pay themselves first before spending all they have on living today. Add to that the cost of leisure and social activities, as well as alcohol, cigarettes, and all of the other *unconscious* spending we do, and it's is no wonder that most people will not have saved enough by retirement to enjoy even a basic standard of living.

The "I don't know where it all went fund "could be the hidden source of most people's financial independence in the future. If you could just put aside a small amount of your "today" money for your future, you would be well on your way to fulfilling your vision for a fantastic retirement.

Our "live for today" attitudes also have adverse effects on our health, because unconsciously spending money on things such as fast food, cigarettes, or alcohol could have a severe impact on our health in the long term. Serious illness can drain us of the energy and resources we need to really enjoy our lives in retirement.

Therefore, by just making small changes and taking "today" money away from unconscious spending and unhealthy living habits and redirecting it toward our future financial independence, we will enjoy more *prosperous* futures, and *healthier* futures as well.

HOW DOES YOUR LIFESTYLE TODAY AFFECT OTHERS?

The life you choose to create for yourself has a significant impact on your whole family as well as you, because if you create an abundance of happiness, love, and money in your life, this will in turn trickle down to all those around you.

Some people say that life is not all about money, and I agree. However, I also believe that a lot of unhappiness and frustration is caused in families by the choices we make with our money.

How many families have been broken because of bad lifestyle choices with money?

Spending all of our disposable income on closets full of clothes that we hardly ever wear, alcohol, cigarettes, gambling, and other reckless behaviors will naturally drain resources from other areas of our lives. This same money could be used to become financially independent or pay off debt that has built up because of the previous bad spending habits in our lives.

By creating compelling visions for our lives and getting on track to attain everything we want out of life, we also set an example to help others imagine new possibilities for their lives, too.

For example, even something as simple as saving 10percent of your monthly income is a lifestyle choice that I wish I had been taught before starting work. If people just did this simple thing with their money right from the start of their working lives, then more people would retire younger and richer than they ever dreamed would be possible. Most people are willing to give big chunks of their money to the lottery every week, hoping that one day "it might be them." I am not suggesting that we shouldn't enjoy ourselves, but just this one simple lifestyle choice could mean a huge difference to you and your family throughout your lives.

To appreciate the long-term impact of this one choice, take out a pen and paper and calculate, to the best of your recollection, how much you have earned each year since you started working. Now multiply that by 10percent. That's how much money you could have sitting in your bank account today. And that's without any interest or the magic of compounding added to it either. Staggering, isn't it?

Think of all the good things you could provide your family once you become financially independent. Think of how your actions could spur on others in your family, your children, and their children after them. What would be possible for them if they learned that by creating compelling futures for themselves, and by making the right lifestyle choices, they too could achieve financial independence, and the freedom to choose how they will spend their time.

THE GREATEST MEASURE OF WEALTH

Most people measure wealth in terms of money. While having an abundance of money is certainly one characteristic of wealth, having an abundance of time is even more important.

In the rat race and humdrum of just getting by these days, most people are losing out on quality time for themselves and their families. It's now the norm for both parents in a family to work, and they often work longer hours than they used to, and take less time off than ever before.

What for?

Is it for fun?

No, it's for making a living and for the quest of money just to pay the bills, and live the lifestyles that we are choosing to live.

Stress is at an all time high in today's manic world, mainly because we don't have the time to rejuvenate and refresh ourselves.

When the day comes to retire, you will then have an additional 8-12 hours of time each day to use. But if you haven't created enough income, you may have all this time but not enough money to enjoy it.

Here is another way to think about the relationship between time and wealth: If you cashed in everything you owned today then paid off all of what you owe, how long would this money last you?

Now, think of this. What if you became financially independent, meaning that the money or assets that you have built up are sufficient enough to provide you with the monthly income you need to live your desired lifestyle for the rest of your life?

Would the money be the greatest asset you have? Or, would it be *the time that this money has bought you* to do what you want, where you want, when you want, and with whom you want—any time you like?

Yes, you may still be busy. But you'd be busy doing things you *want* to do in your life instead of doing things you have to do in order to make ends meet.

WHY WORK FOR THE MONEY?

> *"The master in the art of living makes little distinction between his work and his play, his labor and his leisure, his mind and his body, his information, and his recreation, his love and his religion. He hardly knows which is which. He simply pursues his vision of excellence at whatever he does, leaving others to decide whether he is working or playing. To him he is always doing both"*
>
> —*James Michener*

Why do we work in the jobs or professions that we currently do?

For the majority of people, it is because they finished school and just *drifted* into the work that they are doing. Some people, I realize, *did know* what they wanted to do from a young age, but most of us never considered what we really wanted to do with our lives, because at school, we were never taught how to do what we love to do.

School gave us a minimal general life education, and at best, only prepared us for getting a job of some kind.

With this minimal education, we then start work and start earning money. We have families and need our jobs to support our families and ourselves. We then develop spending habits, and all of a sudden our incomes are fully taken up by our outgoings. So, we strive for promotions or jobs with more pay, so we can keep up, but then we spend more, because our spending habits haven't changed. Then we end up in the same position—again.

OUTGOINGS = INCOME OR MORE, and nothing left over to save.

Are most people who live this way doing what they really enjoy doing?

Are they spending most of their days doing something they love doing, something that really inspires them?

If not, how do we get out of the trap that we find ourselves in, regardless of where we may be in the earnings league?

This is the point where most people may start to think about what they would really love to do with their lives. In most cases, however, they immediately slam the door right in their own faces by listening to the inner voice that says they can't do what they love because they have commitments and need the money to meet them. They need the income that is generated by doing a job they hate just to get by, so they stop dreaming of all the things they would really like to do.

I believe that everyone should have a goal to find work they really love to do. A lucky few stumble into their life's work, but most of us must solve the money puzzle first in order to create the freedom to pursue our heart's desire.

The fact is, hundreds and thousands of ways to create income exist all around us, but we are blind to many of these opportunities, because *we have been conditioned to think that we have to go to work to earn money.* Once you start working on what you love doing, you will find that your energy and enthusiasm grows, and the work you do becomes more exciting. You will start to earn more money than you ever dreamed possible, because you are giving your energy to developing your talents and abilities instead of giving it to a job that you hate. The ultimate irony, of course, is that *by doing what you love, you increase your earning power exponentially.*

"Once the riches start to flow they will come in such abundance that you will wonder where they have been all those lean years." This is the promise that Napoleon Hill made, after stating the importance of setting your major definite purpose, choosing what you want from your life, and then having the persistence to stay with this worthy ideal until it manifests.

In my observation, the truly wealthy people in the world—and I mean wealth in every sense of the word—do what they really want to do and live life on their terms.

What would you be doing with your time today if you were living totally on your own terms and doing what you love?

WHY WORK AT SOMETHING YOU HATE?

"The people who get on in this world are the people who get up and look for the circumstances they want and if they can't find them, make them"

— *George Bernard Shaw*

As I said earlier, most people go to work just because it provides the money they need to get by, pay the bills, and maybe do a few nice things now and again. They work and toil away in these jobs, living payday to payday for forty years, looking forward to the day they can retire and stop doing what they have hated for the majority of their lives. They are counting down the days until their "working hell" is over.

If you look at the wealthy, however, you will see in nearly every case they are working on things that they love to do. They tend to not retire at 65—if they retire at all—because they love doing what they are doing, and they derive tremendous fulfilment from it.

They probably work harder than most because they have the energy that comes from doing what they love to do. They are not working because they have to work to pay the bills—and therefore the work that they do is not really *work* to them; it becomes more of a lifestyle and a hobby.

Just look at people such as Richard Branson, Alan Sugar, Donald Trump, or Bill Gates. Do you think they go to work every day just to earn the money to pay the bills? No, they are working because they love what they do, and the money is just an added bonus that contributes even more value to their lives.

You can look also at people like Ghandi, Mother Theresa or Nelson Mandela. These are people who worked tirelessly, not for money, but because they loved what they did. They were inspired to put their energy toward worthwhile endeavours that ultimately helped millions of people. Do you think they would have wanted to retire at age sixty-five?

Nelson Mandela even became President of South Africa at the age of seventy-five!

It's important to start by imagining—if you weren't working for a pay check—what would you do with the rest of your life that would be worthwhile and fulfilling to both yourself and others?

Would you continue to create even more income through businesses, property, and investments just because you love doing it?

Would you just sit back, take it easy, and take up some hobbies that bring you pleasure or fulfilment?

Would you work in charity or for some cause that provides contribution and benefit not just to yourself but to others as well?

What will you do once you solve your own money puzzle?

> *"I know of no more encouraging fact than the unquestionable ability of man to elevate his life by conscious endeavour"*
>
> *—Henry David Thoreau*

YOUR STARTING POINT TO FINANCIAL INDEPENDENCE

> *"We must start from where we are now, and by rightly estimating our relation to the Divine Universal Mind we can gradually grow into any conditions we desire, provided we first make ourselves in habitual mental attitude the person who corresponds to those conditions"*
>
> *– Thomas Troward*

When planning to become financially independent, it's imperative to understand your current position in relation to your long-term financial goals. Only when you have acknowledged your present reality can you begin to work out an actionable plan that will get you where you want to be.

Knowing that you want to get to Paris but not knowing whether you are in London, New York, or Sydney is the same as knowing you want to become financially free but not knowing if you are massively in debt, spending too much of your money unconsciously, or have assets and skills that you can use to jump start your path to financial freedom.

Once you know your starting point and your end goal, then there are many ways you can take to get there—just as if you are in London and want to get to Paris; you could drive, go by coach, train, aeroplane, or boat. You could even walk if you had the time or energy!

There is a famous saying that "The truth will set you free," and this is critical to remember when it comes to achieving financial goals. You need to know exactly where you are with your money, as this information holds the power to clarify the right choices that will move you closer to creating the life of your dreams. For example:

- You need to know exactly where you are earning your money from, how this is taxed, and how much of what you earn you actually take home.
- You need to know how much you owe, how much interest you are paying, and how much your debt is really costing you.
- You need to know what you own, how much your assets are worth, what your real assets are, and how these can be leveraged to improve your standard of living in the future.
- You need to know exactly what your current retirement provision will provide for you when you retire and when it will provide it.
- You need to know what your current beliefs are regarding money, as well as what beliefs you hold about yourself as someone who can generate large sums of money.
- You need to know where you are currently getting your financial advice from and where this advice is leading you.
- And, perhaps most importantly, you need to know:

    ✓ Where you are spending your money
    ✓ When you are spending it
    ✓ Why you are spending it

Where you are now is the result of all the actions you have taken in the past. The past does not have to equal the future, but you can only change course if you're willing to make the necessary changes to become financially independent.

Gerry Robert said in his book, *The Millionaire Mindset—How Ordinary People Create Extraordinary Income*

"Good ideas are shot down by people who assume the future is an extension of the past—the past does not equal the future."

Knowledge is the key to a new and better future.

EVERY GOAL MUST BE FUNDED

Every goal, dream, or desire requires money in order to come to fruition. Regardless of your specific goal, you need income to be able to realize it. It's easy to see how purely material goals such as buying a car, a home, or a fancy new wardrobe require money to fulfil, but even more esoteric goals have a price— be it in terms of money or time.

For instance, if your goal is to take a year off work to travel the world, then you need both the money to pay for the actual travel but also the money to replace the "time cost" of not working for a year.

Some short-term goals, such as sitting quietly to meditate each day or going for a run four times per week entail only a "time cost." But if you decided to go on a month-long meditation retreat or run the New York marathon, then these would involve a "financial cost" as well.

So, if we agree that all goals need an income in order to be realized, then we can actually start to quantify how much income we need to create in order to become financially independent and to live the life that we truly desire.

I once heard a great quote that said something like "most people think that they'll need far more than they do to become financially independent, and actually settle for a lot less." I interpret this to mean that if only people realized how little it would actually take for them to be financially free, more and more people would be inspired to create the life of their dreams instead of sitting back and letting life pass them by, hoping to make ends meet both during and after their working lives.

Once you know how much you need in order to live the life you really want to live, then you can start considering all the options available to you to build the resources and the money you require. Unless you can quantify these things, any financial goals you do make will not be understood in the proper context.

There is no point in setting a goal to create 1 million in net worth and a 200,000 dollar per year income unless you know what this will do for you. It has no meaning until you assign a meaning to it, and you can only appreciate what that money will do for you after you've taken the time to clarify and design the lifestyle that you really want.

HOW MUCH WILL YOU NEED?

> *"In the long run, men hit only what they aim at. Therefore, they had better aim at something high"*
>
> —*Henry David Thoreau*

It is so important to know with as much accuracy as possible how much money you need to become financially independent. There is no point guessing what you'll need, as you will probably end up way, way short when the time comes. Most people do not even realize what their current retirement provision will give them when they finish work, and they just assume they'll be ok. When it's explained to them that their income will fall in retirement, most people's attitude is, "Oh well, I won't need as much by then anyway."

This is all just guessing, and guessing will never provide the financial security that is needed later in life. If we just took the time to work out how much we will actually need to live the lives we want to live, we would know exactly how much we will need and what we'll need to do to create it.

If you knew you were going away for a weekend, you would pack enough clothes for a few days. If you knew you were going away for a week, you would pack enough for a week, and if you knew you were going away for a year, then you would pack enough for a year. If you were building a house and you knew you would need —let's say—5,000 bricks, you wouldn't just order 3,000 bricks from the merchant and hope for the best, would you?

Becoming financially independent is a very scientific thing—you find out how much you'll need and set about building it. It's as simple as that. Now, everyone is different, and your amount will be a unique reflection of the kind of lifestyle you want to create.

That's what is absolutely great about planning financial independence; it's totally up to you!

WHEN DO YOU WANT IT?

Determining *when* you want to become financially independent is as important as knowing *how much* you need to become financially independent. Knowing the timescale that you want to achieve your goal by will help you determine the best route forward. If you know that you have thirty years until you want to retire or become financially independent, you can take a different route than if you have only five years.

By knowing your starting position, how much you need, and by when need it, you can work out what return per year you need on your assets to truly create the life of your dreams.

Most people do not even think about when they want to retire. They just go along someone else's path until they are allowed or told to retire—and as a result, they are not in any way in control over their own destinies. By working out what, when, and how much you need to become financially independent by the time you retire, you will be light years ahead of the majority of people in planning for a fulfilling future.

YOUR LIFE VISION AND GOALS EXERCISE

The creative process that you are now going to undertake could well be the most beneficial time you have ever spent. You need to set aside a few hours or even a day in order to fully gain the benefit of this powerful exercise. Setting *goals* for our lives is the single most important thing we can do to ensure our lives are exciting and have meaning. The particular journey you embark on once your goal has been set becomes as exhilarating as reaching the goal itself.

Most of us set goals by accident rather than by design. We often set them on a reactive basis rather than proactively thinking about what we truly want out of life. For example, X happens and we don't like it and decide that we want Y instead. Or X happens, and we like it a lot and decide we want more of X.

What we often fail to understand is that whether we are *proactively* setting goals or *reactively* setting goals, we are designing our lives. It's the difference between being the pilot of an airplane taking off with a planned destination or taking off with no planned destination.

The pilot with a planned destination knows where he is going and can make decisions en route to alter his course to make sure he stays on track and arrives at his destination. The pilot with no planned destination will have no idea where he intends to land and will make decisions based on how he feels in the moment, on what the weather's like, or on how much fuel he has left.

Both planes may end up arriving in the same place, but which one would you prefer to book your ticket with?

Decide upon the lifestyle you want both for today and for your future. This will depend on a variety of thing, such as the type of home you want to live in, the type of education you might want for your children, the car you want to drive, the vacations or holidays you want to have, the clothes you want to wear, or maybe the amount you want to donate back to charitable organizations.

> *Caution—you may get caught in the trap of thinking about what you can afford rather than what you want. This is not the idea. This process is about designing the life you want, not the life you think you can afford based on your current conditioning. You don't have to know how you might achieve these things yet— that's not for consideration at this stage.*

Your goals must be specific and should always be something you *want*, and not something you *need*. There is no inspiration in *needs*. There is only inspiration in *wants*. Goals do not have to be *logical*, and in fact, it is more likely that you will be inspired to action if it is totally illogical. Saying that you are going to earn 3percent more income from your job and retire at age sixty-five is a very logical goal, but it really isn't that inspiring. Whereas, setting a goal to start a business that will help thousands, or millions of people in the world, and that will also enable you to retire at the age of forty-five with a 1 million dollar income is a much more inspiring goal. Or, saying that you will lose one pound of weight next year is hardly likely to cause massive action to make the necessary changes to your lifestyle. Setting a goal to lose twenty pounds of weight and create an outstandingly fit body before you go on vacation in six months is far more likely to inspire the action necessary for you to fulfil your desire for a new you.

You do not need to know how you will achieve your goals. In fact, if you are already aware of how you will achieve your goals then they are probably not big enough goals for you to really grow in life.

When creating your life vision, the first thing to do is to decide upon what categories are important for you to feel fulfilled and successful. There are many different areas of our lives that we can look at, whether it is in our personal lives or professional lives, and your categories may be slightly different from someone else's. Everyone's life is based on their own unique experiences, and so you have to decide for yourself the areas you want to focus on in order to become a consciously pro-active goal setter and achiever. Some areas you might want to consider are the six areas of life that Anthony Robbins uses in his Wheel of Life: *physical, emotional, financial, family, spiritual,* and *career.* James Ray uses a similar set of categories in his Harmonic Wealth Programs: *physical, spiritual, financial, relational,* AND *mental.* Here's a list of life categories that may help you decide what areas of your life you most want to improve:

- **Outstanding Family and Home Life**
- **Superb Health and Fitness**
- **Fantastic Business and Work Life**
- **Wonderful Leisure Time**
- **Emotional and Mental Strength**
- **Continuous Personal Growth and Development**
- **Marvellous Toys and Things To Own**
- **Absolute Financial Freedom**

What are the categories of your life that most you want to improve?

Category 1	Category 6
Category 2	Category 7
Category 3	Category 8
Category 4	Category 9
Category 5	Category 10

Great! Now that you have chosen the aspects of your life that you want to improve, let's set off on the creative process of designing your life exactly the way you desire it to be. To do this, I am going to ask you to imagine your ideal scenario in each area of your life, determine what you will need to do in order to achieve this vision, and understand the costs that will be required to realize your goals and desires. Remember, once you know *what* you want and *why* you want it, the *how* becomes much easier.

Reflect on each category that you identified above, then repeat this process for each one.

YOUR SUCCESSES

What *successes* have you already created in this area of your life?

1.	6.
2.	7.
3.	8.
4.	9.
5.	10.

YOUR STRENGTHS AND ABILITIES

What are your main *strengths and abilities* in *this* area of your life?

1.	6.
2.	7.
3.	8.
4.	9.
5.	10.

YOUR PERCEIVED WEAKNESSES

What are your *perceived weaknesses* in this area of your life?

1.	6.
2.	7.
3.	8.
4.	9.
5.	10.

YOUR IDEAL VISION

If this area of your life were absolutely perfect in every way, what would it look like? What is your *ideal vision* in this category?

HOW WILL THIS IDEAL VISION BENEFIT YOU?

What *benefits* will you notice once you are living your *ideal vision* in this area of your life?

1.	6.
2.	7.
3.	8.
4.	9.
5.	10.

WHO ELSE WILL BENEFIT FROM YOUR IDEAL VISION?

Who else will *benefit* from you creating your *ideal vision* in this area of your life?

1.	6.
2.	7.
3.	8.
4.	9.
5.	10.

HOW WILL YOU FEEL?

How will *you feel* when you are living your *ideal vision* in this area of your life?

ASSESSING YOURSELF IN RELATION TO YOUR IDEAL VISION

On a scale of 0–10 (with 10 being that you are already living your *ideal vision*), what number would you give yourself to represent how close you are to living your *ideal vision* in this area of your life?

0	1	2	3	4	5	6	7	8	9
10									

WHY DID YOU CHOOSE THIS NUMBER?

Why did you choose this number and not lower on the scale of 0–10?	

What resources, skills, and abilities do you already possess that caused you to rate yourself at this number?	1. 2. 3. 4. 5. 6. 7. 8. 9. 10.
What would have to happen in your life right now for you to move up just one point on the scale of 0–10?	
What is the next step you can take in order to realize your *ideal vision* in this area of your life?	

RESOURCES, SKILLS AND KNOWLEDGE

What *resources, skills, or knowledge* do you feel you need most in order to *create* your *ideal vision* in this area of your life?

1.	6.
2.	7.
3.	8.
4.	9.
5.	10.

YOUR MOST DESIRED GOALS

What are your *ten most desired goals* in this area of your life? If you knew that it was *impossible to fail,* that your life was *perfect,* and that you have *unlimited money, time, talent, abilities, and support from your family and friends,* what would you *choose to create* in this category?

1.	
2.	
3.	
4.	
5.	
6.	
7.	
8.	
9.	
10.	

WHY DO YOU WANT TO ACHIEVE YOUR MOST DESIRED GOALS?

For each of your ten most desired goals, write a statement that expresses *why you want this* in your life.

MOST DESIRED GOAL	WHY DO YOU WANT THIS?
1.	
2.	
3.	
4.	
5.	
6.	
7.	
8.	
9.	
10.	

WHAT ARE YOUR MOST IMPORTANT GOALS?

Prioritize your list from 1–10. What is *most important* for you to *achieve* in this area of your life?

1.
2.
3.
4.
5.
6.
7.
8.
9.
10.

WHAT IS THE MONETARY COST?

What will be the *monetary cost* of creating your *most desired goals* in this area of your life? For example, if your goal is to live in a 1 million dollar home, you would have to work out whether you are going to buy this in cash, which would require a capital investment of $1 million. You would also need to calculate how much it would cost to maintain this kind of home, and how much the running costs such as electricity, gas, and property taxes would be per year. This would give you the annual cost of fulfilling your goal. If you would need a mortgage to help you finance the purchase, then this would obviously make the capital cost of the goal less but push up your annual cost, because you'd have to make your mortgage payments as well as cover the running costs. If you had a goal of going on a no-expense-spared round the world trip, you would have to work out how much this trip would cost you in total, and that would be your capital cost of the goal. There would be no annual cost of the goal, as this would be a onetime trip. However, if you had a goal of spending six weeks of every year visiting five-star luxury resorts around the world, this would generate an annual cost, but no one-time capital investment. Finally, if you wanted to have a full body massage and facial once a week, every week, then you would have an annual cost to calculate for achieving this goal with no upfront capital costs. Once you can calculate exactly how much it will cost you in terms of capital and ongoing costs in order to achieve all of your goals in life, it is much easier to find the best strategies for creating the money in order to achieve all your dreams and desires.

MOST DESIRED GOAL	CAPITAL COST OF GOAL	ANNUAL COST OF GOAL
1.		
2.		
3.		
4.		
5.		
6.		
7.		
8.		
9.		
10.		

WHAT IS THE TIME COST?

What will be the *time* cost of creating your *most desired goals* in this area of your life?

MOST DESIRED GOAL	TIME COST
1.	
2.	
3.	
4.	
5.	
6.	
7.	
8.	
9.	
10.	

TWO KEY ACTIONS

What are *two key actions* that you *must take* to *achieve* your *most desired goals* for your Category 1 area?

MOST DESIRED GOAL	2 KEY ACTIONS
1.	1. 2.
2.	1. 2.
3.	1. 2.
4.	1. 2.
5.	1. 2.
6.	1. 2.
7.	1. 2.
8.	1. 2.
9.	1. 2.
10.	1. 2.

Now that you have created your goals for the major areas of your life, you need to know your starting position. By identifying your starting point and your final destination, you can plan the most effective route to realize your desires.

Complete the following financial statement to reveal exactly where you are in your life right now.

Income	Expenditures
Salary—	Home Mortgage—
	Council/Property Tax—
Rental Income—	Income Tax—
	Health Insurance—
Dividends—	Utilities—
	Car Payment—
Interest from Savings—	Fuel—
	Car Maintenance—
Business Income—	Car Insurance—
	Life Insurance—
Pension/Retirement Income—	Income Protection—
	Critical Illness Protection—
Other—	Food /Home—
	Food /Eating Out—
Total =	Credit Cards—
	Store Cards—
	Personal Loans—
	Business Loans—
	Other Mortgages—
	Entertainment—
	Grooming—
	Holidays/Vacations—
	Birthdays—
	Christmas—
	Smoking—
	Alcohol—
	Subscriptions—
	Pension/Retirement Contributions—

	Regular Savings— Contributions/Charity— Other Spending Money— Total =
Assets	Liabilities
Home—	Home Mortgage—
Property—	Other Mortgages—
Stocks and Shares—	Credit Cards—
Savings—	Store Cards—
Business Assets—	Personal Loans—
Pension Fund Value—	Business Loans—
Total =	Total =

Although it takes time and consideration to translate the silent wishes of your heart onto paper, the moment you do, you exponentially increase the likelihood of them coming to fruition. At the same time, the moment you can examine your current financial situation on paper in black and white, you will be that much more motivated to make better choices for your future.

It may be easier to just skip past these exercises, but I highly encourage you to take some time and answer these questions. Unless you actually decide what it is you want, how can you possibly achieve it? And, unless you accurately understand your current financial position today, it is far more difficult to choose the best strategies for creating what you truly want in the future.

By clearly identifying your starting point and your ultimate destination, the path to get there will light up in front of you!

MONEY PUZZLE MASTERY EXERCISES—
WHAT DO YOU WANT?

After reading this chapter and seriously thinking about its content, what three things are most important for you to remember about how to create what you want in your life?

1. _____
2. _____
3. _____

How has learning this affected the way you think about your financial future?

_____
_____
_____
_____

What actions do you intend to take from what you have learned in this chapter in order to create a more successful and abundant future?

1. _____
2. _____
3. _____
4. _____
5. _____

4

MONEY

> *"Money will have a greater influence on your life than almost any other commodity you can think of"*
>
> —*Bob Proctor*

WHAT IS MONEY?

N O one would argue the power that money holds over us or the way it can influence our lives and the lives of those around us. Learning to harness this power for our own benefit is essential for our financial solvency, and to do this, we must understand what money is—and what it's not.

So what is money anyway?

Money is really only an idea, a human invention that we made up and manufactured thousands of years ago. Money really isn't the paper or coins that we pass from one hand to another. These are merely symbols that facilitate the exchanging of goods and services. Money is a servant that we employ in order to make ourselves and others comfortable.

Too many of us have assigned to money a great power that controls how we feel and what we do in our lives. Humans have killed for money, enslaved for money, stolen for money, abused for money, sold drugs for money, been unhappy because of money, been fearful because of money, and enslaved themselves in an endless grind —all in pursuit of money. We have allowed money to dictate the terms of how we live our lives and to determine the choices we make. Dreams, too, are shelved out of the fear that we don't have enough money to pursue them.

Vicki Robin, in her book *Your Money or Your Life* writes about people who, instead of making a living at their work, more accurately "make a dying," or, in some cases, "make a killing." The work they're doing is unfulfilling, perhaps even detrimental to their own or others' well-being. Or, perhaps they're embarrassed about their work. They hate it. They wish they didn't have to do it. They pretend that it doesn't matter, when in actuality, their pursuit of money may result in the killing off of their spirit or someone else's spirit. Caught up in the chase, they say they are making a living, when they are really making a dying or a killing, but they don't see it, they *don't want* to see it, or they can't admit it.

Money is neutral. It can be used for both good and bad in the same way that a knife can be used to cut your food or to kill someone. It is the intent behind our use of money that gives money its power.

Money can be a vehicle to fulfil our greatest dreams and highest ideals in life. By becoming financially independent—meaning that we have built up sufficient assets to provide for our basic expenses without having to work for it ourselves— we open ourselves up to finding work that brings us fulfilment while making the world a better place for those around us to enjoy.

HOW CAN WE CREATE MONEY?

Now we know that money is just a vehicle for fulfilling our dreams and desires. The next thing to consider is—how do we earn it?

We are not taught about money in school—neither how to earn it nor how to wisely spend it. The whole school system is set up to teach people how to become employees, and that is why the majority of people get jobs when they leave school. Usually we take our first jobs between the ages of sixteen and twenty-one, or sometimes a little later, depending on our education and the length of time required to learn a profession or trade. Most people drift into these jobs without having considered the countless other options available for earning money and without considering whether or not the job that they have chosen is one they will enjoy doing for the rest of their lives.

Before they know it, they are in the rat race: They get married, buy a home, start a family, and spend every bit of money they've got coming in, trying to keep pace with the cost of living. They then strive to earn more, but the more they earn, the more they spend, and soon they are back to square one with all of their money being spent.

They might save a little, and they might even be putting a little towards their pension or retirement fund—something they think they should be doing—but without really knowing why.

TIME FOR MONEY

The basic misconception about the job scenario as a means to earn income is that *it assumes we must trade our time for money*. Let's think about this for a moment. If we are trading our time for money, then by how much can we really hope to increase our income levels? And how much influence do we really have on our own earning power if we must rely on someone else to employ us?

The answer to both of these points is clearly very little, regardless of whether you are earning $10 per hour, $50 per hour, or $200 per hour, because if your pay depends on the amount of time that you trade to earn it, then you are capped by the amount of time that you can give. We can influence our pay by improving our skills or working hard to gain promotions or higher pay, but in the end there will be a limit as to how much we can earn if we are still exchanging our time for money.

It doesn't matter whether you are male or female, black or white, educated or uneducated, tall or short, fat or slim; you only have 24 hours in a day, 168 hours per week, or 8736 hours per year. Even if you allowed only 8 hours for sleeping per day, 2 hours for eating, 1 hour for driving and did nothing else but work the rest of time, at a rate of $10 per hour, the maximum you could earn is $47,320 per year. At $50 per hour, your annual income would be $236,600. Now, that may sound like a lot of money, but the cost of reaching this goal is not one that most people would be willing to pay.

Also, by working for someone else, you are totally controlled as to what you earn, and for how long you earn it. There is no guarantee that your employer, in this day and age, will keep paying you forever, and a job for life is no longer a realistic scenario or a comfort that you can rely upon.

Why then do the majority of people still trade their time for money and still operate under the belief that this is the most effective way of creating financial security? The main reason is the fact that most people are unaware of the countless other channels through which money can flow.

MONEY FOR MONEY

If trading your time for money has been your primary strategy, here is another possibility to consider: putting your money to work for money. When you put your money to work for money, you are actually using the *energy of money*, rather than only using your own energy to create more money.

Now, in this scenario is there a limit as to how much income you can create?

Absolutely NOT!

There may be a limit to how much you start with, but there is absolutely no limit on the amount you can accumulate over time.

In this scenario, are you under the control of an employer or the limited number of hours in a day as to how much you can earn?

Absolutely NOT!

It is totally and completely up to you as to how much you make. The beauty of having money work for you rather than you working for money is that it doesn't matter if you are working, sleeping, eating, or lazing on the beach, your money will still be working. Once you have built up enough money so that the income that is generated is sufficient to cover your expenses, you will have reached the point where you never have to work for money again.

Most people think that investing money is risky and having a job is secure, but as you can see from the scenarios above, it is completely the other way around.

OTHER PEOPLE'S TIME FOR MONEY

Another way of earning money is by having other people's time earn you money. This is where you employ other people to generate income. You pay them a salary or commission for doing so, and earn a profit on all that they make you.

For example, if you sell widgets and you manage to sell 100 widgets a week from using your own time and effort and earn a profit of $5 per widget, then you would make $500 per week profit. However, if you were to employ another person to sell 100 widgets, and paid them $3 for every one they sold, this would still leave you with $2 per widget profit, which translates into $200 per week.

Therefore, just by employing one person and using one other person's time and effort, you have increased your profit by 40%!! And what's more you haven't done anything yourself, apart from sourcing the widgets in the first place—all in all not a bad weeks work!

Now, is there a limit on the amount of money you could make in this scenario?

Absolutely NOT!

The amount of money you will make will depend on how many people you want to employ to sell your widgets. For example, you would only need three employees to earn more money than you were generating by trading your own time for money, and at this point you no longer have to trade your time for money ever again.

What if you employed 100 people? That's $20,000 per week profit! And you haven't spent any of your own time generating this!!

MULTIPLE SOURCES OF INCOME

When you learn how to leverage your time, your money, other people's time, and finally other people's money, there is no limit to the income you can generate. This is the secret to how the wealthy always seem to get wealthier—they have money flowing to them from multiple sources.

The more sources of income you can generate in your life, the more secure you will be because if one source of income slows down, falls or even disappears, then you have other sources of income to fall back on for security.

You will never create multiple sources of income just by trading your own time for money. The best way to create wealth is to create multiple sources of income through using your time, your money, other people's time, and other people's money.

THE TWO PURPOSES OF MONEY

Money has two basic purposes: The first aim of money is to make you more comfortable in life. The more money you have, the more basic needs you can satisfy, and the more comfortable your life will be. You can live in a more comfortable home, eat better, have more clothes, and travel more comfortably when you have more money. You can also enjoy more leisure time and participate in more activities that make your life comfortable. You can rest more, exercise more, and go on more vacations. And of course, when you are rested and comfortable you are more productive, and you may even feel happier. While we're on the subject, I'd like to touch upon the connection between money and happiness.

We've all heard the expression that "Money cannot buy you happiness." Let's get this straight. Money was never meant to make you happy. This is as ridiculous a statement as saying, "you can't drive your fridge to the supermarket." You were never meant to drive your fridge to the supermarket—it's meant to keep your food chilled.

Money is meant to make you more comfortable, not happy, and the consolation is that even if you are miserable, having more money will at least make you more comfortable in your misery.

Money provides you with the ability to live life to the fullest in body by eating good food, wearing comfortable clothing, having a comfortable and warm place to live, and the resources to be free from excessive toil in life.

Money provides you with the ability to live life to the fullest in mind by providing the capability to buy books and the time to read and study them; and the opportunity to travel and see all the beauty one is capable of appreciating in the world.

Money also provides the ability to live life to the fullest in soul, and to do this we must experience love. In his book, *The Science of Getting Rich*, Wallace Wattles said that:

"Our highest happiness is found in the bestowal of benefits on those we love. Love finds its most natural and spontaneous expression in giving. And the expression of love is often frustrated by poverty. When we have nothing to give, we cannot fill the place as a spouse, a parent, as a citizen, or as a human being."

I don't believe that "empty gifts" are what Wattles was referring to here, but rather the fulfilment that we can create when we give of our hearts, our thoughts, and our time. These are the most valuable gifts we can offer another; yet we can't share them unless we have a measure of wealth. Seen in this light, money is a beautiful tool that enables us to bring comfort, material security, and love to ourselves, our families, and our surroundings.

The second aim of money is to help us extend our service far beyond the boundaries of our own presence. The more money you have, the broader your sphere of influence, and the bigger a game you can afford to play. There is only so much comfort that we can enjoy in our lives; at some point it becomes excessive. Hoarding money for one's own benefit and gratification is a great misuse of its power.

There is an old saying and belief that the "rich are greedy." On the whole this is completely untrue, as some of the wealthiest people on the planet are the most generous with their money, and can, because of their great wealth, contribute far more than someone who has limited resources. It is true that some rich people are greedy, but isn't it equally true that some poor people are also greedy?

MONEY IS A MAGNIFIER

If you are a greedy person, a nasty person, a hateful person, or a paranoid person who thinks that everyone is out to get you, having more money will likely magnify these qualities within your character. So too, if you a nice person, a sharing person, a loving person, or a trusting person who thinks the world is out to help you, then money will accentuate these qualities as well. Money does not create character; it's the person who creates the character.

We cannot take money with us when we die, but the more wealth we create in our lives, the bigger the legacy we can leave behind—the more we can share and contribute to others, and the greater the impact we can have on our family, our community, and our world.

Andrew Carnegie, the Scottish-born American industrialist, businessman, and major philanthropist who died in 1919, once said that his goal was to spend the first half of his life making a huge amount of money, and the second half of his life giving it all away. What a great goal to have in life! Even though he is considered by many as one of the richest men in history, he contributed in ways that never would have been possible had he not made his fortunes.

With the fortune he made from business, he turned to philanthropy and education, founding the Carnegie Corporation of New York, Carnegie Endowment for International Peace, and Carnegie Mellon University in Pittsburgh. While Carnegie paid his employees the low wages typical of the time, he later gave away most of his money to fund the establishment of many libraries, schools, and universities in America, the United Kingdom, and other countries, as well as a pension fund for former employees.

We have similar people in our world today who are living their lives with the same generous spirit. Richard Branson, Bill Gates, John Templeton, and Warren Buffet are among the wealthiest people in recent history, and have also been huge philanthropists and humanitarians who have given away enormous amounts of their wealth for the greater good of mankind.

USING MONEY WITH INTENT

Using money to contribute to others is not limited to only the wealthy; every one of us has this ability. Money is just a form of energy, and the intention we put behind our giving can infuse it with far more value than just the dollar amount.

In her wonderful book, *The Soul of Money*, Lynne Twist tells a fantastic story about when she first started fundraising for The Hunger Project. While on a trip to New York, she met with the CEO of a large corporation that had just received some very bad press. In a token gesture to redeem the company's soiled public image, the executive handed her a check for $50,000.

Lynne left her meeting in the Manhattan penthouse offices to get to her next fundraiser, which was taking place in an old church building in Harlem. The surroundings couldn't have provided a more stark contrast from where she had just been. Lynne knew that the 75 or so people who had gathered for the fundraising event did not have much money to give; nonetheless, she told them about the mission of The Hunger Project, and then she made her plea for donations.

The room fell silent and after a while a woman toward the back of the room stood up. "Girl," she began, "My name is Gertrude. I like what you've said, and I like you. Now, I ain't got no check book, and I ain't got no credit cards. To me, money is like water. For some it rushes through their life like a raging river. Money comes through my life like a little trickle. But I want to pass it on in a way that does most good for the most folks. I see that as my right and my responsibility. It's also my joy. I have fifty dollars in my purse that I earned from doing a white woman's wash, and I want to give it to you."

And with that, the woman walked forward and handed Lynn her fifty dollars. One by one, other people came forward, and in total Lynn collected about $500 from a group of people who lived in one of the poorest areas of New York. Yet there was more power in this group's $500—initiated by Gertrude giving an entire day's wages—than there was in the strategic and loveless $50,000 check that she had been presented with hours earlier.

In this scenario, whose money was given with the most powerful intent, and which giver do you think will ultimately benefit the most? Was it the CEO with the guilty conscience and millions to play with, or Gertrude, with very little resources, but a beautiful attitude and positive intention to help others?

The end of this story, by the way, is that Lynn gave the $50,000 back to the CEO, along with a letter explaining that they did not want to accept dirty money from a company trying to clean up its image. Years later, however, this same CEO retired with a handsome benefits package from his company, and chose to donate over $50,000 from his own pocket to The Hunger Project, explaining that his earlier encounter with Lynne showed him that he did, in fact, want to contribute to ending world hunger.

You see, it is not all about money. It's about intent. If we can endow our giving with the underlying intent that it contributes to those who receive it, this intent will become magnified and will return to us in ways we cannot begin to imagine.

FINANCIAL EDUCATION WILL FREE YOU FROM POVERTY

Financial education is the key that can free you from potential poverty in retirement. In educating ourselves about how to better plan for our futures, we unlock the power to control our own financial destinies, rather than leaving it in the hands of others to decide our futures.

Unfortunately, with the exception of learning how to count it, very few of us received any education about money in school. We were simply never taught how to make money, how to get our money working for us, how to avoid debt, build assets, manage cash flow, or any of the other essential skills that we need to create a life of financial independence.

Without this knowledge, we cannot hope to do anything different than what we are already doing, and this is why the vast majority of people still follow the same financial paths that were taken by their parents and grandparents, who lived in a totally different world when it comes to money, retirement, and economy than we live in today.

We have to take responsibility for our own futures now, and education is the first step. We have to take the time to understand money, retirement, investing, setting and achieving goals, creating financial leverage, and making better financial decisions. If we plod on through our lives without learning new strategies to help us build wealth in retirement, then we could end up seriously short of money, and may end up having to keep working long after we'd like—just to keep food on our tables and roofs over our heads.

By gaining a financial education and taking the right steps early enough, we can free ourselves from the risk of running out of money in retirement, and can plan for a financially secure and independent future.

We are living in a new and changing economy that necessitates a new way of thinking, planning, and managing our money. We cannot make new decisions and think new thoughts based upon an old paradigm of beliefs about money and retirement. Therefore, it is vital that you get the right financial education, so you can move forward intelligently in this new and rapidly changing economy.

The good news is that you have at your fingertips far more opportunity and information than ever before to become financially independent by the time you reach retirement. You need only to formulate a plan that will allow you to analyze where you are now, so you can adjust your actions accordingly in the months and years ahead. And for this, you've come to the right place!

> *"The strongest force in the human personality is the need to remain consistent with how we define ourselves"*
>
> —*Anthony Robbins*

TEN PERCENT TO FINANCIAL FREEDOM

The main reason that people don't become financially independent is that they don't keep enough of the money they earn to build a financial money mountain that will then generate their future income and make them financially secure.

As Robert Kiyosaki noted:

"Most people fail to realize that in life, it's not how much money you make, it's how much you keep."

If we only realized early on how important it is to pay ourselves before spending our money on anything else! When we try to save money from what we have left over after we've fulfilled all of our other commitments, too often we find that there is nothing left at the end of the month to save. Whereas, if the first person we paid at the start of the month were ourselves, then we could happily spend everything else we earned, knowing quite well that we have at least made another step towards a financially secure future.

We must develop the habit of paying ourselves first, otherwise it won't take long before our outgoings and spending habits make it difficult—if not impossible— to save for our futures.

Unconscious spending habits and the ever-growing "I don't know where it all went fund" are robbing us of the ability to create lives of financial independence.

When I first learned these things, I analyzed my own situation and calculated the amount of money I would have saved since starting to earn, if I had known about this "Pay Yourself First" strategy all along. It frightened me to the core when I worked it out, and I'm sharing it here so that maybe, just maybe, you will see the light and start saving at least 10 percent of your income from here on out!

Between the times when I started working until the day I did this exercise, I estimated that I had earned roughly £487,000. Had I saved just 10percent of this income with a 5percent per annum return since day one, I would have built up a total of £62,000.

This £62,000, if wisely invested, could have then bought me assets worth over £412,000. We will discuss financial leverage a little later, but for now, I want to just highlight how quickly assets can be built just by saving 10percent of your income.

In a twenty-year period, assuming that these assets grew by just 5percent per year, they would be worth over £1 million, giving me a net equity value of nearly £800,000 that I could do what I like with!

I urge you to get a pen and paper and work out for yourself how much you would have saved if you had paid yourself 10percent of your income. This will definitely inspire you to start today, and get on the path to financial freedom, I promise!!

Financial well-being starts with personal responsibility, and the very first place we must start exercising this power is by affecting our own spending habits. You must be the one to decide to start applying the 10percent rule to every dollar you earn. Although it can be difficult in the moment, as soon as you realize the effect that this one healthy habit can have on your long-term financial well-being, you'll be motivated to keep travelling on the road to financial independence.

KEEP YOUR MONEY FLOWING—THE LAW OF ENERGY

> *"No one speaks of creating energy, but only of transforming one form of energy into another"*
>
> —*Thomas Troward*

Everything is energy.

Every *atom* that makes up every *molecule* that makes up every bit of *matter* is *energy*. They are all vibrating, electromagnetic waves of light, called *quanta*. Quantum physics has revealed that even the things that appear to be solid— your car, your house, a tree, this book, and even you—are not solid at all. On the quantum level, everything in our world is comprised of impulses of energy and information, and is made up of 99.9999999 percent light—in other words—*energy*.

All energy vibrates at a particular frequency. The difference between physical things and non-physical things is the frequency at which they vibrate. Energies that vibrate at the same frequency will resonate and gravitate toward one another, while energies that have dissimilar frequencies will be repelled away from one another.

Our thoughts are also waves of energy. Much like a radio has to be tuned into the frequency of the station that you want to hear, you have to be tuned into the results you want to create in your life, and the way to do this is to tune your thoughts and intentions to the frequency of already having what you want.

The more positive our thoughts are, the more easily we will attract positive experiences into our lives. Conversely, the more negative our thoughts are, the more we will attract negative experiences into our lives.

What has also been revealed is that energy is always moving, and nothing stays the same. In fact, change is all there is. Everything in our world is either growing or dying; expanding or disintegrating. In every second of our existence tens of thousands of our body's cells die, and in the next second, tens of thousands of new cells are created. In fact, every cell in our body is replaced in less than a year, so you aren't even the same physical person you were a year ago.

John Assaraf's program, *Mindset for Success* demonstrates that:

- Energy is neither created nor destroyed
- Energy is the cause and effect of itself
- Energy is evenly present at all places at all times
- Energy is in constant motion and never rests
- Energy is forever moving from one form to another
- Change is energy's only attribute
- Energy is *everything*!

If everything is energy, then what is money? It's *energy*, of course.

If energy's only attributes are that it continually changes form and exists in a state of perpetual motion, then doesn't it make sense to keep money moving and flowing in our lives?

Keeping money moving will create more money because of the law of energy. If anything in life is allowed to stand idle, then it will start to erode. If you doubt this, just think about the health of a couch potato, a car that is left outside without being driven for months, or a pool of stagnant water that is left to attract germs.

I remember one day wondering why the Dead Sea is called the Dead Sea. I did a little research and discovered that all of the rivers that flow into the Dead Sea are alive and vibrant, but as soon as they merge into one body of water, the current stops flowing, and sure enough, it loses all its vibrancy and life, and becomes dead.

It's the same with money. If you keep money moving by investing in assets that will continue to grow, your finances will remain alive and healthy, and you will create more money in the future. But if you allow money to just sit in one place, its real value will erode over time and could, like the Dead Sea, stop flowing altogether.

Let's look at an example of someone who has $50,000 in a bank account and is afraid of doing anything with this money for fear of losing it. He leaves his money sitting in his savings account year after year after year after year. He may be getting paid interest on his money, but after you deduct tax from the amount he earns and then take inflation (the rising cost of living) into account, you will find that in ten years his money is not worth much more in real terms than it is today; in fact, it could well be worth less.

Now, imagine someone else with this same $50,000, but instead of leaving it sitting idly in his account, this person decides to put it into motion by investing it in a piece of property. By using leverage (which we'll discuss later in more detail), this person would be able to purchase approximately $333,000 worth of property with his $50,000. Let's also say that he doesn't do anything else with this money over the next ten years.

Do you think that $333,000 worth of property will be worth more or less in ten years than the $50,000 sitting in a bank account? Of course, it will be worth more.

However, once this person has leveraged his $50,000 into a property, that equity—or money-making energy—must be kept circulating. Too often, people who own their own homes allow their equity to stagnate rather than putting it to work for them—just like the man in the previous example who kept his money sitting in the bank. Why tie up your equity in just one house, when it could be used to buy additional assets that will propel you towards financial independence?

I have used property as an example here to demonstrate why it is better to invest your money rather than let it stagnate and erode in value over time. The same $50,000 could have been used for all sorts of different things, such as starting a business, buying shares, investing in your education, or creating multiple sources of income. All of these things would keep your money flowing, circulating, and accumulating

WHERE DOES MONEY FLOW?

Knowing how money flows in and out of your life is vitally important when building a wealthy retirement, because, as Robert Kiyosaki says many times in his books, "Cash flow is king."

To gain a firm understanding of where your money is flowing from and where it is going to, you have to look at the facts in the four main areas of your financial life.

These four areas are:

Income

Expenditure

Assets

Liabilities

Once you put all the facts down on paper and have listed all the numbers in each category, you can then start to see where your money is flowing currently, and how it might flow in the future when calculating what your retirement will look like. This is the first step to getting your money flowing in a way that can create real wealth.

Analyzing all of the areas of your financial life, and knowing where the cash flows in each area will illuminate the reality of your life situation, and it can be a very enlightening experience. People soon realize that what they thought was their biggest asset—their home—is most often their biggest liability, because it drains them of cash flow, and does little to improve their long term wealth if it is the only property they ever own.

You will also realize that thanks to taxes, the income you earn as an employee flows very quickly from the income column to the expense column.

Projecting this forward, you will soon realize that most of the expenses you have will still be there when you retire, and the income you will receive from your pension will reduce. Therefore, your cash flow and standard of living will suffer in the future.

Another sobering experience that comes out of analyzing the four areas of your financial life is seeing on paper the cash that flows out each month, without you realizing where it goes.

The insidious nature of unconscious spending habits causes cash to flow right out of our pockets into the world of spend, spend, spend instead of flowing to things that will increase our wealth, and provide more spending power for us in the future.

CREATING YOUR MONEY MOUNTAIN

Building your money mountain is vitally important to creating financial freedom, because it puts you in total control over what you do in your life, in terms of both work and leisure.

As long as you are relying on getting your income from a *job*, then you are totally under the control of somebody else with regard to how much you get paid, and even if you get paid at all. No job can be guaranteed these days, and therefore your income will only last for as long as your employer is willing to keep paying you.

Relying solely on a job for your income is also very risky from the viewpoint of health, as you can only earn income from your employer if your health allows you to work. If your health should suffer, your employer may pay you for a while, you may have some income protection policy that will pay you a portion of your previous earnings, and you may get some benefits from the state.

However, if your income came not solely from a job, but from the money mountain that you have created for yourself, it would not matter if you were working or not, as your income each month would still flow to you no matter what.

When you have money paying you, rather than you having to trade your time for it, you are in a much more secure financial position in life. Also, if you are focused on building money to create your income in the future, then you are not limited by anyone or anything in how much income you can earn in the future—the only limit is the size of the money mountain you build, and that is totally up to you!!

FINANCIAL INDEPENDENCE SHOULD BE EVERYONE'S FIRST GOAL IN LIFE

Volumes have been written about goal setting, and I do firmly believe that setting goals for ourselves and making plans to achieve them is one of the most powerful things we can do. If we don't know what we want, and we don't plan to get them, then how on earth will we ever achieve anything different than we already have?

However, I also believe that setting too many goals can become confusing—therefore it's wise to focus on what's most important for a reasonable length of time.

In *Think and Grow Rich,* Napoleon Hill said that it is vitally important to have a definite chief aim in life, meaning to have one goal that you focus on more than anything else until you succeed. And your financial independence is the one main goal that is definitely worth your continued focus.

Once you solve your own personal money puzzle, you gain the freedom to do whatever you want from that point forward. Because the fulfilment of any goal has a money component, achieving the money to pursue our dreams should be of paramount importance.

The one caveat to this that I would like to stress is that although becoming financially independent should be everyone's definite chief aim in life, we should never get so focused on making money that we neglect the other important parts of our lives. Too many people have watched their marriages fail, their kids grow up to be strangers, and their health deteriorate as they pursued money just for money's sake. I don't think that anyone gets to the end of their life and wishes he'd spent more time in the office.

This is why you must create a compelling vision for your life to begin with. If you go off pursuing money based solely on the "*got to have more*" mentality, then this will cause you to neglect other really important things in life and may even cause you to lose what it is you were working towards in the first place.

So, remember, even though it is vitally important that you focus on creating the wealth in your life that will make you and your family more comfortable and secure in the future, you must still devote time in the present for your children, spouse, family, health, fun, relaxation, and contribution. Then you will have a truly prosperous and wealthy life in all areas.

WHAT WE FOCUS ON GROWS

> *"Focus is the ultimate power that can change the way we think, the way we feel, and what we do in any moment. When we change our focus, we change our lives. What we focus on determines the direction in which we move"*
>
> —*Anthony Robbins*

When starting to consider retirement planning and saving for their futures, the majority of people focus on their lack of money. This prevents them from really making a start on creating a truly wealthy future.

The problem with this thinking is that the more we focus on the lack of money in our lives, the more lack we will attract into our lives.

The recent film, *The Secret,* brought the Law of Attraction—a topic that has been taught for decades and written about for well over a century—to the mainstream. This universal principle explains how, through the conduit of our thoughts, ideas, beliefs, and actions, the unseen world gives rise to the circumstances and events of our lives.

It was Isaac Newton who first introduced the principle of Cause and Effect when seeking to understand the physical, mechanical world, noting that "Every action has an equal and opposite reaction." Quantum scientists have now discovered that Newton's law of Cause and Effect does not apply only to the physical, mechanical world, but also to the mechanics of everything, including our thoughts.

> *"If we regard the fulfilment of our purpose as contingent upon any circumstances, past, present, or future, we are not making use of first cause; we have descended to the level of secondary causation, which is the region of doubts, fears, and limitations, all of which we are impressing upon the universal subjective mind with the inevitable result that it will build up corresponding external conditions. But if we realize that the region of secondary causes is the region of mere reflections we shall not think of our purpose as contingent on any conditions whatever, but shall know that by forming the idea of it in the absolute, and maintaining that idea, we have shaped the first cause into the desired form and can await the result with cheerful expectancy"*
>
> —*Thomas Troward*

We create the circumstances of our own lives—including the circumstances surrounding our current financial situations— through the quality of our own thoughts, behaviors, and actions. Most of us, however, try to change the effect without first looking at the cause: *ourselves*. Understanding the cause and effect relationship between our thoughts and the results we create provides two important benefits: First, it affirms that because we are free to choose our own thoughts, actions, and behaviors, we alone have control of the results we achieve in life. Second, it eliminates the thought that things just happen to us, because we are victims, and shows us that we are capable of creating the results that we truly want to create. To put this law to work for us, we have to practice attuning our thoughts, beliefs, and ideas to the goals we want to achieve.

Inherent within The Law of Attraction is something called the "Law of Resonance." This principle states that in the same way a tuning fork will vibrate in harmony with whatever note is played on a piano or other musical instrument, we can learn to align our thoughts to harmonize with the outcomes we want to generate in our lives.

The events and circumstances we draw to us are always a direct result of where our thoughts are focused; what we focus on expands, grows stronger, and multiplies. By focusing on what we *do have* rather than what we lack, we summon the full power of our wealth building potential. This is the secret to retiring in financial abundance rather than financial lack.

Anthony Robbins used a great metaphor for the power of focus when he described how he learned to drive a race car around a track. Before he set off, the teacher taught him that if the car were to go into a high speed spin, then all he would have to do is focus his attention on the track, and his body would adjust the steering wheel accordingly to get him headed back in the right direction. The first time he went off, guess what happened? Sure enough, he went into a high speed spin. But instead of listening to the instructor and focusing his attention on the track, all he could focus on was the wall that he was going to crash into. And, of course, by focusing on the wall, his body started guiding the car straight toward it. Luckily, his instructor was with him and got him out of the spin and back on the track. Time after time, the same thing happened: he would spin, focus on the wall, head for the wall, and his instructor would get him out of trouble. The third or fourth time this happened, however, he made an important shift in his attention and instead of focusing on the wall, he focused on the track.

So, while the car was spinning, his eyes were firmly fixed on the track and where he wanted to be. Lo and behold, his body made the right adjustments, and before he knew it, he was back on the track and speeding around with a newfound confidence in his ability to influence the outcome of his life by focusing on the direction he wanted to go, rather than where he didn't.

To apply this lesson to your own life, begin to notice the ways that your thoughts may be taking you into the wall, so to speak, and away from the track. Here are some questions that will help:

- Are you focusing on what you want or on what you don't want?
- Are you focusing on what you have or on what you don't have?
- Do you spend more time worrying about the debt you've accumulated or appreciating the abundance of ideas and resources that are available to help you create more in your life?

THERE IS ENOUGH ABUNDANCE IN THE WORLD FOR EVERYONE

Much of the doubt that we feel about our ability to create abundance in our lives stems, I believe, from the fear that there is not enough money for us all to become truly wealthy.

The fact is that there are more than enough resources in the world for every single person on this planet to be wealthy. It's true that there are many people in the world living in dire conditions, lacking food, shelter, freedom, and opportunity. However, if you look around, you will find there are a huge number of people who are living in a state of affluence compared with the really poor in our world. They have more money, more clothes, more food, more cars, more toys, more education, more opportunity, more comfort, and basically more of everything.

It's ironic that in our world of plenty, the majority of our conversations and complaints tend to center on what we lack and what we don't have enough of. Robert Holden, in his book *Success Intelligence*, cited the results of a recent poll carried out in America, where people were asked how much money it would take for them to feel satisfied. Those earning $30,000 per year said they would need $50,000 to feel totally satisfied. The poll then asked people who earned $100,000 per year the same question. They said that they would need $250,000 a year to feel satisfied in life. Guess what people who earned $250,000 said?

"I don't have enough money. I don't have enough time. I don't have enough

sleep. I don't have enough leisure. I don't earn enough profits. I'm not thin enough, smart enough, fit enough, or educated enough—and I certainly am not rich enough."

This is the mentality of a vast majority of people who live in circumstances of absolute luxury and comfort, compared to many millions of people around the world who really don't have enough of the basic things in life to make themselves safe or comfortable.

This inner feeling of scarcity and lack infuses fear into our perceptions about money. The fear of not having enough leads many of us to believe that others are out to take advantage of us financially or that if we're not careful, we will lose what is rightfully ours.

Time and time again, I have seen people descend into a downward spiral of fear about money until eventually they come to perceive everything in life as "us vs. them," or what I call a "you *or* me" mentality. When we view life in these terms, it's very difficult to have faith that there are more than enough resources to go around, or to envision win-win solutions where everyone benefits. Money, opportunity, success, happiness, food, water, land, housing, and everything else that sustains us are available in great abundance. These resources are like the air we breathe that keeps us alive every day, and at the same time sustains billions of other people.

Just take in a deep breath—right now. You took in every bit of air that you needed from the abundant supply that is available. Did that leave me with not enough air, or your spouse, or your next door neighbor, or someone living thousands of miles away from you? Absolutely not! You took everything you needed from the abundant supply, and still the abundant supply remained.

Lack of money and resources has never been our problem; it's a lack of ideas that prevents us from achieving anything we want in our lives.

Take a look around, and you will see that everything you interact with—whether a person or a material object—began as an idea in someone's mind that eventually manifested into a reality. This is true of the current models of financial planning that the majority of people follow today.

So, even if we do not *currently* have the money we wish to have, we all have the capability to generate ideas that could be leveraged to create financially independent futures. Because we all have the ability to expand the limitations of our own thinking, the opportunities are boundless for each us of to more effectively utilize our own resources, and use what we already have to create more abundance in our lives.

Anthony Robbins once said that the more we help others get what *they* want in life then the more *we* will get. If you use your mind effectively to think of ways to be more productive and of greater service in your life, you open the door for greater quantities of abundance to flow to you.

THE MAGIC OF COMPOUND INTEREST

It was Einstein who once said that compound interest was the Eighth Wonder of the World. When it comes to making money, I really believe that compound interest is one of most potent forces on earth. The growth of your money will continue to escalate in an upward trend if only you will allow your investments the time to grow.

If I were to offer you the choice of receiving either $10,000 in your hand today or $1, doubled every day for the next fifteen days, what would your first reaction be? Without understanding the power of compounding you would probably snap my hand off for the $10,000. On day two you would still be laughing at me, waving the $10,000 in my face to prove how you had outsmarted me, as choosing the second option would have given only $2 at this point. On the third day you would have had only $4, so you'd still be feeling smug with your $10,000. The fourth day you would have had $8, and by day ten you would have earned $512 ... And you are still laughing all the way to the bank with your $10,000. But here's where the power of compounding starts to take effect. On day eleven you would have earned $1024; on day twelve, $2048, on day thirteen, $4096, and on day 14, $8192, which is still less than $10K, so you'd probably still feel confident with your choice. However, if you had gone the route of earning compound interest rather than taking the cash in hand, on the fifteenth day, your payment would now be $16,384! So, by waiting fifteen days and delaying your gratification in order to allow the power of compounding to take effect, you would receive over 60 percent more money than by jumping in and taking your return without giving compound interest time to *exponentially increase* the growth of your money.

Time is your friend when it comes to compound interest, so being patient, delaying gratification, and allowing compound interest to have its way with your money will help you to master your wealth building potential.

THE LAW OF INCREASING RETURN

Like compound interest, being generous with your money has the power to increase your abundance, because of a principle called "The Law of Increasing Returns."

When a farmer sows a seed in the ground and cultivates it until harvest time, the Law of Increasing Returns brings him back not only the original seed he planted but a many-fold increase.

Henry Ford understood the Law of Increasing Returns in the early 1900s when, in 1914, he offered his workers a $5 per day wage, which more than doubled their earnings. Did he do this to be a great philanthropist, or just because he wanted to be generous? No, he did it because by paying a better than average wage, he received better than average service from his employees—and this helped him to attract the best labor in the market.

This move turned out to become very profitable for Mr. Ford, and he referred to his "wage motive" as a sure-fire way to get the best from his employees. If you are constantly looking at ways to provide more service and contribute to others, then the Law of Increasing Returns will bring more back to you in greater quantities than that with which you began.

Too many people today are working from the reverse strategy: they expect results or money without doing that which is necessary to attain them.

It is our "entitlement" consciousness that leads us to believe that we should receive without first giving of ourselves. Make it your business to render more service and better service than that which you are paid for, and your harvest will be one like the farmer sowing his crops. The seeds that you plant, the service that you render, and the generosity that you have with your money will, come harvest time, reap many-fold rewards beyond your original actions. There is a great poem in Bob Proctor's book, *You Were Born Rich,* which sums up the Law of Increasing Returns. It's called "Giving," and was written by Arthur William Beer:

GIVING

To get he had tried,
Yet his store was still meagre.
To a wise man he cried,
In a voice keen and eager;
Pray tell me how I may successfully live?
And the wise man replied,
"To get you must give."

As to giving he said,
"What have I to give?"
I've scarce enough bread,
And of course one must live;
But I would partake of Life's bountiful store.
Came the wise man's response;
"Then you must give more."

The lesson he learned;
To get was forgotten,
Toward mankind he turned
With a love new begotten.
As he gave of himself in useful living,
Then joy crowned his days,
For he grew rich in giving.

MONEY PUZZLE MASTERY EXERCISES—MONEY

After reading this chapter and seriously thinking about its content, what three things are most important for you to remember about *money?*

1. _____
2. _____
3. _____

How has learning this affected the way you think about your financial future?

_____
_____
_____
_____

As a result of what you have learned in this chapter, what actions do you intend to take in order to create a more successful and abundant future?

1. _____
2. _____
3. _____
4. _____
5. _____

What were you taught about money in school?

_____
_____
_____
_____

What are your thoughts about why you go to work, and the differences between the various ways we trade our time, money, or others' money for money?

_____
_____
_____
_____

How much money do you think it would take for you to really feel satisfied today?

_____
_____
_____
_____

5

TIME

> *"This is the beginning of a new day. God has given me this day to use as I will. I can waste it or use it for good. What I do today is very important because I am exchanging a day of my life for it. When tomorrow comes, this day will be gone forever. Leaving something in its place something I have traded for it. I want it to be a gain, not loss—good, not evil—success, not failure—in order that I shall not forget the price I paid for it"*
>
> —*Paul Bryant*

GIVE YOURSELF THE TIME TO CREATE

GIVING yourself the time to create what you want in your life is vital to your success. Without the time to think about what you really want—free from all other distractions—how can you expect to create a plan for achieving whatever it is that you truly desire?

The majority of people say they haven't got the time to do many things, especially to set goals, and plan their lives. And yet these people have exactly the same amount of time as anyone else in life, from the laziest person to the most industrious person.

The fact is that we all have exactly 24 hours in every day and 168 hours in every week. It doesn't matter whether you are the President of the United States, the CEO of a major organization, a top sports star, a bestselling author, a home-maker, or an unemployed couch potato. It's still the same—24 hours in a day, every day—and 168 hours in a week, every week.

It's what we do with our time that counts, and the activities we pursue with our time that have the ability to change our lives. It has been said that we spend more time each year planning our vacations or Christmas than we do in planning our dreams, goals, and desires in life. This is sad, because our annual vacation or Christmas each year are just fleeting occurrences that come and go, and while they are usually enjoyable, surely our lives, our dreams, and our goals are more important. Surely *we* are more important!

Just think what you could achieve if you broke free from the hum-drum of your usual routine and the monotonous chores that occupy your attention each day, and set aside *just a few of those hours* to focus on *yourself* and what *you really want to create.*

Without this dedicated time, all of your dreams and aspirations will remain as fantasies and wishes, floating about in the dark corners of your mind. But by creating the time and focus to clarify what you want, you transform these idle fantasies into clear and specific goals that you can set out to achieve.

This is my pet theory, actually, about why so much money is spent on the lottery each week. It's easier to spend a minute or two filling out a form, crossing out numbers, and silently hoping that "It could be me!" as we hand over the slip to the cashier. This may be easy on our time but is it realistic? Well, for the extremely small percentage who win, I suppose it is, but for the rest of us, the answer is a resounding "No!"

We have to make the commitment to get ourselves off the treadmill long enough and often enough to ask ourselves what it is we really want from our lives. The following are some good questions to get you started:

- What do we want to achieve in our lives?
- What do we want to become in our lives?
- What do we want to have in our lives?
- What do we want to learn?
- Where do we want to go?
- Who do we want to meet?
- Where do we want to work?
- How do we want to earn our money?
- Where would we like to spend our leisure time?
- Who would we like to spend our leisure time with?
- How would we like to contribute to the world?

By becoming really clear about what you want, you will unleash the inspiration to make new choices and ultimately, to alter the course of your life completely.

For the next thirty days, I challenge you to take an hour each week to focus only on yourself—I call this "me time"—where you think deeply about what you truly desire in life. I guarantee this will be the best investment you ever make. There is no substitute for taking the time to clarify the direction you want your life to take —it's the only way you'll be able to create a reliable plan for achieving your goals.

SELF CONTROL

> *"Do not squander time, for that is the stuff life is made of"*
> —*Benjamin Franklin*

In actuality, you have all the time you need to do everything it will take to become successful. The difference between living a life of chaos and a life of harmony is developing self-control as to how to spend your time. Earl Nightingale once said, "you cannot manage the time you have, you can only manage what activities you do with the time you've got."

As I said before, we are all given the same twenty-four hours each day, but it's up to us to have self-control over what we do in each of these hours. Each second, minute, hour, or day that we spend is gone the moment we've spent it. We cannot get it back, other than in the form of memories.

So, instead of spending hours in front of the TV, hours on the Internet "surfing," hours in the bar, or playing the Xbox or Wii, wouldn't our time be better spent deciding what we want for our lives and then planning our activities to achieve those goals?

Developing self-control over the ways we spend our time is vital to building up the resources we will need to live comfortably in retirement. The people who go through life wasting their time on activities that don't move them forward are usually the same people who will get to retirement and look back at all the time they've wasted and lives that have passed them by, wondering how it could have been different if only they had spent their time more wisely.

Time is a priceless commodity and our biggest asset. Tragically, it is also our most wasted resource. Money can always be made, but time can't be bought at any price. One person could have a million pounds and another only ten pounds, but if a doctor gave them both six months to live, they would still have only six months, and no money in the world will change this fact.

However, it is true that money and time are intrinsically linked: The time we invest in building our resources in the present creates the money that will free up our time in the future. And of course, having money is what will enable us to enjoy more of our time once we retire.

Let's say two people were to retire at 65 years of age, and both are to live until 100 (not an uncommon occurrence these days, as centenarians are one of the fastest growing segments of our population!). These two people have exactly 35 years— or 306,600 hours— left to live. Who do you think will live the more comfortable life? The person who from the age of 30 decided to take control over his time, and devote an hour a week to learning about money and investing his time in building assets for his retirement, or the person who spent all of his life from 30 on in front of the TV, surfing the net, or drinking in bars and clubs with his mates? You decide.

Both of these individuals have the same amount of time left, but choices made early on will determine to a large extent whether that time will be spent enjoying life to its fullest, or struggling just to get by.

TIME IS CRITICAL IN BUILDING LONG TERM WEALTH

Giving your investments time to grow is critical to building long-term equity and wealth, because the effects of compounding over time will escalate your wealth like a snowball. As we saw earlier, the effect of compounding is dramatic once given time to work its magic. Imagine if you had given up on day ten: You would have walked away with $512. But, by being patient and giving your money time to grow until day twenty, this $512 would have turned into over $524,000. Not a bad return for eight days of patience!

Let's look at another example. Imagine that you are just starting out, and you buy a property worth $100,000 in today's market. Let's say this property appreciates in value at 10percent per year. In year one, the value of the property will grow by $10,000; by year five, the annual growth will have grown to $14,641; by year ten, the annual growth will have grown by a further $23,579k, and by year twenty-five by another $98,497k. This is from the same starting value of $100,000 and the same growth rate each year, but as you can see, the growth each year doesn't rise steadily. The growth escalates and escalates, and the growth in year twenty-five is 885percent higher than the growth in year one!

We live in a fast-paced world, and most of us have fallen into the trap of looking for faster and faster ways to do things. We multi-task to fit more activity into our days, eat fast food on the run, shop by internet, date by phone, text message friends and loved ones instead of having conversations with them, and get up early to the sound of our alarms to start another manic day on the go, grabbing breakfast in the car or not at all. There just never seems to be enough time.

Far too many people invest their money in the same hurried way, expecting fast returns, and hoping to make a quick buck.

I can tell you that in the long run, moving from one investment to another, hoping to make some quick returns will not give you the results you are seeking. You have to take your time and allow the power of compounding growth to work for you.

You also need to take your time to make sure that the investment you are making is a sound one, and then, once all factors have been taken into account, and the decision has been made, you need to leave your investments to grow. In time, the affects of compounding will provide you with the real returns that you are looking for.

Let's take property as an example. If you look at property values in the U.S since 1963, and in the U.K. since 1946, you will see that the average ten-year growth since then has been 92percent and 140percent respectively. So if you bought a property a year ago and it hasn't grown enough in your eyes to have made you the fast buck you were looking for, then be patient. Ten years from now, if the growth rate is the same as it has been over the past ten years, it will likely be worth a great deal more than it is today!

Even if current property trends might be sideways or slightly down in value, by being patient, you will ride out the peaks and troughs, and the long term effect will be equity growth and greater wealth in the future.

The magic of compounding proves why time and patience is so important. It also shows why it is essential not to delay, and to start building wealth as early as possible in life. The more time we have to allow the wonderful effects of compounding to make a real difference in our lives, the greater our wealth will be.

Anthony Robbins said that the most successful people in life are those who make decisions rapidly, and are slow to reverse a well-thought-out position. Conversely, he says that people who fail usually decide slowly and change their minds frequently. All of this means that once you have made a sound decision, stick with it, give it time, and the rewards will pay off.

CREATE A TIMELINE FOR YOUR LIFE

A timeline is an exercise where you get a blank piece of paper and draw a line from left to right on the page. On the left hand side you can write the word *now* and also your current age. The further right you go depicts time moving forward in your life until you get to the farthest point on the right, which depicts the end of your life.

In between, you can then mark out all of the events that are likely to occur, and at what approximate age. For example, you could write in age sixty-five as the age you plan to retire, age fifty-five as when you expect to pay off your home mortgage, age forty-eight when your first child becomes eighteen, and may go to a university, and the dates when you'll celebrate your silver, ruby, or golden wedding anniversaries. This timeline can also be a place for you to map out all of the other goals you will set for yourself along the way.

So, if one of your goals is to take a year off work and travel the world, then you can start to plan *when* along the timeline you'd like this to occur. Anything and everything you can think of for your life can be recorded on your timeline, and this is a fantastic way of mapping out what you want to do, and approximately when you want to do it. It's also a powerful way of helping you to realize how much money you will need, and by when you will need it.

The timeline process is an effective tool for future planning for several reasons:

Firstly, because the human brain thinks in pictures, drawing out something on paper that reflects the events and milestones of what you want and expect for your life will help you formulate a clearer idea of exactly how you want things to unfold. Once this picture is clear, you can then determine how much time you actually have to set about making it happen.

Secondly, creating a timeline for your life can reveal the true reality of how long you have to go before you retire or before certain events may happen in your life. Too many people leave planning for the future until it is far too late, and then find they don't have enough time to achieve the outcomes they had hoped to create for themselves or for their families.

Thirdly, creating a timeline for your life can help you prepare not only for the probable events like wedding anniversaries, daughters getting married, retirement, and children going to on to college, but for your less obvious dreams and desires as well. Once you have set out what it is that you truly want in life, a timeline can help you visualize the point at which you'd like to achieve certain goals. This process can and will be very powerful.

Fourthly, creating a timeline for your life will highlight the number of pay days you have left before you are due to retire. This in itself can be quite startling, as it reveals how many chances you really have left to start building the funds that will be required in order to retire comfortably. For example, if somebody is forty-five years of age and has a goal to retire by age sixty, drawing out her timeline will reveal that there are only 180 pay days (assuming that this person gets paid monthly) left until retirement. And, every month that passes means there are fewer and fewer opportunities for her to take meaningful action.

Fifthly, creating a timeline for your life can also help you realize how financial leverage can help your money grow far quicker when buying assets for retirement planning rather than just saving some money each month out of your salary.

Finally, creating a timeline is a great way to divide your life into different segments, and this too can help you in the process of long term planning. You will also realize that potentially one of the longest segments of your life will be the segment after you retire, and this awareness can be transformational in the sense that it may strengthen your commitment to create enough money, not only to survive, but to truly enjoy your retirement.

MAKE WORK MORE ENJOYABLE

Work becomes a joy rather than an obligation once you know what it is you are working toward. When you have a purpose in life, a vision for what you want to achieve, and know why you want to achieve it, work becomes fun, and the time you spend working seems to just whizz by.

I think this is why some of the most successful people in the world have always worked way past the traditional retirement age of sixty-five. They love what they do and see the greater purpose it serves, so the time they spend "working" becomes irrelevant, because they are having fun doing it.

In 1996, George Burns, the famous American comedian and actor, died at the age of 100. He worked right up to the last few years of his life, and was as beloved in the last two decades of his life as he was at any other time during his career. Bobby Robson, the soccer manager who took England to the brink of the 1990 World Cup Final, was appointed manager of Newcastle United at the age of sixty-six, and managed them until the age of seventy-one. Did he finish here? No, he then went on to be appointed as a consultant to the Republic of Ireland Manager Steve Staunton, at the age of seventy-two.

Do you think that George Burns or Bobby Robson worked because they had to, or because they loved what they did and had a great vision for their work? There are many, many other examples of truly inspired people with such a big visions, that age and time are simply are not limiting factors. Mother Theresa worked until shortly before her death at the age of eighty-seven. At the time of this writing, Nelson Mandela is ninety years of age, and is still actively contributing to the world—and this is after having spent twenty-seven years of his life in prison.

When we are free to work at something we love to do rather than work at something because we have to, life becomes truly inspiring. Working toward a worthy ideal is the closest I think you get to becoming truly successful in life. Time passes joyfully rather than monotonously, and even though you will still come across challenges and problems, you are better able to deal with these when you are inspired by a great vision.

TIME FOR LEISURE—A COSTLY TIME

Outside of the regular bills that go out each month, when do we spend the majority of our money? It's in our leisure time, of course. So what can we expect to happen when the time comes to finish work and retire?

The reality is, we are going to have a lot more leisure time on our hands to fill. Without enough money, the problem could be that we will have too much time to fill without the resources to fully enjoy ourselves in retirement. And, having worked for thirty or forty years, who in their right mind would not want to enjoy themselves when they are now free to do so?

This points to a problem that few of us anticipate while we are still in our earning years: Many people, especially those with final salary pension schemes, know they are going to get only a certain percentage of their final earnings as pension. They have acclimated to the fact that having less in retirement is the norm, and have resigned themselves to having to adapt their lifestyles to much lower income levels. Why settle for less though? Especially when our leisure time increases so much!

Work this out: You work for forty hours a week for thirty years. How much free time have you enjoyed throughout all these years?

If you're lucky, you've had two or three hours a day to yourself before you have to sleep in order to wake up to go to work again. And then maybe, if you're lucky, you get eight or ten hours on the weekend—that is, if you haven't brought any work home with you. So, maybe you have had thirty-five hours per week for leisure in total. And this is without the chores that need doing around the house!

Let's say you have finished work and are one of the lucky ones who is with a company that still provides a pension that is equivalent of $1/60^{th}$ of your final salary for every year that you worked. You will finish work on $30/60^{ths}$ of your final salary. That's half of what you were earning! But, what's happened to your leisure time?

It has risen from thirty-five hours per week to seventy hours per week, and you now have ten hours of leisure time to fill every day. So, your leisure time has doubled, but your income to enjoy this leisure time has halved. This just doesn't make sense.

So, when you truly grasp that it is in your leisure time that you spend your money, and that your leisure time dramatically increases when you finish work, this should inspire you to look at your financial planning for retirement a lot more carefully. It should motivate you to begin to build greater resources so that you do not finish work without the money you need to enjoy yourself fully and live your life in the most fantastic way possible.

The arrival of retirement will find you in one of two categories: either you are prepared or you are unprepared.

For the prepared, retirement can be a time for more opportunity, a time for planning, a time for comfort, and a time for luxury. It can be a time of great enjoyment, of travel, of spending quality time with those we love. It can also be a great time for sharing all the gifts that we have built up over the years. It can be a time of contentment and of great pride in what we have achieved so far in our lives.

For the unprepared, the arrival of retirement is more likely to be a time of regret and sorrow, a time of uncertainty and struggle—a time when we will ask, "what if"? What if we had been more disciplined earlier in life? What if we had used our time more effectively and our resources more fully? What if we had started earlier to build the money we needed to fund a more enjoyable retirement, free from worry and stress?

Anticipating these scenes in advance can provide you with the inspiration to do what you need to do now to create the life you really desire for your retirement. Time is your most valuable resource. Don't let it slip away.

FREE YOUR TIME TO DO THE THINGS YOU LOVE

> *"You will be amazed at how much free time you actually have when you never have to think about or worry about money"*
>
> —*Bob Proctor*

Freeing your time to do the things that you love to do is a wonderful goal for anyone to have. It will lead to a richer and more fulfilled life that is full of enthusiasm and enjoyment. Far too many people drift from school into jobs that don't really inspire them, simply because it's what they believe they should do or must do in order to pay the bills.

One of my clients recently told me that she wished she had followed her heart when she was younger and gone to fashion school, as her passion was designing dresses. Instead, she followed the advice of her teachers and her parents and ended up becoming a school teacher. For years she hasn't had much enthusiasm and felt as if she was still following someone else's dreams rather than her own. After we created a plan for her to build wealth by utilizing her own talents and natural interests, she created a goal to start up an internet business designing girls' dresses. She has since realized that her real desire is to leave the job she doesn't feel inspired to do and to start doing something that brings her joy.

Her enthusiasm for life has been renewed as she is now following her own plan. This is already giving her a far richer experience of life, and instead of drudging away at a job she hates, she is following her own dreams and desires.

How many people in the world are in a similar position? Toiling away at jobs they hate and that don't inspire them in any way, while all the while their own dreams and plans are lying dormant inside them. Tragically, unless they set aside the time now to discover what their heart truly desires, these dreams will never become a reality.

Too many people, having suppressed their own wishes and lived their life according to someone else's plan, "die with their music still inside." You only get one life and it's not a dress rehearsal, so why not set about freeing your time up in order to truly live the way you want to, and make your life as rich an experience as you possibly can?

> *"A life of fulfilment is one in which we put urgency in its place and remember that the ultimate target is to spend our lives doing the things that we believe are most important to us"*
>
> —*Anthony Robbins*

THE COMMITMENTS ON OUR TIME

To be truly successful, you have to take into consideration all areas of your life. Success isn't just about money; it's also about creating happy and fulfilling relationships, enjoying great physical and mental health, and continuing to grow personally, professionally, and emotionally year after year. Because the true measure of success means fulfilling goals in multiple dimensions of your life, you will naturally have commitments on your time in each of these key areas. But how many of your time commitments are a reflection of someone else's expectation, rather than a reflection of your own desires?

Most people claim they haven't got time to do the things they really want to do, but upon deeper reflection, find that some of these commitments do not really serve them in the long run. The TV, the football match, the hour spent reading the newspaper each day—these are all commitments, or habits, that we have built up over the years, but are they really taking us where we want to go?

Could our time be spent more wisely? Is spending that hour on the internet better for us than spending time planning how we could make more of our lives?

Would our time be better spent going to seminars on how we could invest better for our futures? Or would it be better spent in the pub talking to all the same people about how bad things are in the world financially, socially, or politically?

Once you analyze the commitments in your life right now, you can start to identify the ones that serve you and your future and reduce or discard the ones that are not supporting your life's aims. You can free up time to start working on your plan for financial freedom.

Once you have set aside the time to work on what you want and know why you want it, creating the time to actually make it happen becomes infinitely easier. Remember, when you have a great purpose in life and a big enough *why*, the *how* starts to take care of itself. Can you sit down and give yourself the time to work out what it is that you want? Or, are you using your current time commitments as an excuse to avoid planning your future?

In the end, we all have the same number of hours in a day, and we'll all have the same number of hours in a day when we retire. It's just the way that we'll be able to spend our time that will be different!

THE TIME TO LEARN

The old saying "Knowledge is Power" is so true, and when it comes to money, finances, and retirement funds, knowledge is *everything*.

The sad reality is that most people still believe someone else will look after them in retirement, so they don't feel the need to learn how to look after themselves. If they had taken the time to learn about retirement, they would soon realize that today's world demands all of us to take complete responsibility for own financial futures. This new knowledge would give them the power to identify the resources they will need in order to make a real difference in their financial futures.

Setting aside time to learn is a critical part of success. Unless we learn skills for the future, we are setting ourselves up to get left behind in the past. Making the time to learn is also vital for personal growth. The world is moving on at such a fast pace that unless we find the time to learn, how can we ever expect to keep up? I once heard a great quote from Charlie 'Tremendous' Jones that said "You will be exactly the same person in five years' time as you are now, except for the books you read and the people you meet." It's true that unless we expand our knowledge, we will never really see any personal growth in our lives.

By giving yourself time to learn the art of making money, managing your finances, and creating real wealth, you will build the confidence necessary to take action. Once you have taken action you then have practical experience to add to theoretical education. This leads to more understanding, which leads to more skill, and inevitably to increased knowledge and confidence.

Most people think that investing is risky. Believe me, it's not.

However, investing your money without first investing in your financial education *is* risky, and that's why most people get burned when they invest. They listen to their financial advisers who say to put their money in a particular retirement plan, bond, unit trust, or mutual fund. They don't know any better, so they follow the advice. The stock market plummets, and they lose money. Or they buy a hot stock tip from a magazine or from a friend. They know nothing about the company or why it could go up, but they invest anyway. The stock never goes up or falls, and they lose money. Or, they buy a property because the newspapers are filled with stories of house price increases, only to find that they have bought the wrong property, and it won't rent—and they lose money.

Taking the time to educate yourself about the risks and trends that could affect your wealth, and learning safe investment strategies to build your future financial security are vital steps in your overall financial plan. Therefore, set aside the time now to learn and grow and to acquire the knowledge you need to become financially independent.

It could be the most productive time you ever spend!

PATIENCE AND TIME

There are several reasons why people often lack the patience to stick with a financial plan long enough for it to be successful:

Firstly, instead of patiently creating our lives with careful thought, too often we get distracted by the next rosy looking opportunity. We go off on a tangent and before we know it, we have lost focus on what we originally set out to achieve.

We are bombarded with empty opportunities promising us quick money and get-rich-quick schemes. Because our fast-paced world trains us to think in terms of instant results, it's easy to fall prey to scams that promise us a fortune without any effort and planning. This could be why so many millions are spent each week on lotteries around the world. Everyone wants their riches *now,* but few have the patience to construct realistic plans to create them.

Remember, the most successful people are those who are slow to reverse a well thought out position. If you want to create real wealth in your life, you have to have to give your plans the time that they need to really work for you.

Lack of faith is the second reason that people rarely stick with their plans long enough to achieve success. They lack faith in their abilities, and they lack faith in themselves to make the right financial choices, so they simply hand over the reins of their financial planning to institutions such as banks and insurance companies, which they believe to be "experts" when it comes to managing their money.

Lack of faith causes us to second guess ourselves and change course mid-stream. It also makes us highly susceptible to unfounded information we hear from the media, from friends, family members, and from perfect strangers. This may explain why so many people still believe that traditional methods of investing are the most reliable, even when all evidence proves otherwise. Lack of faith, combined with lack of financial savvy, seduces us into following the crowd: we get a job, buy a house, pay into a retirement fund, get bombarded by advertising, and spend most of our money on things that don't really matter. We are encouraged from multiple sources to invest our money in banks or financial institutions that we hope will one day look after us in our old age.

Finally, I believe that many people fail to realize their financial plans because that they lack the persistence needed to become successful. The majority of people give up far too soon on their dreams and desires, and if they had persisted that little bit longer, they would probably have seen success unfold like never before.

The essence of persistence is in having will power, and if you combine a strong will with a strong desire and a belief in yourself, there is nothing to stop you from creating any form of riches you want to in your life.

How many diets do people start and then stop too soon?

How many exercise regimes do people start and then stop too soon?

And how many dreams or ideas do we think of, that are too quickly pushed to the back of our minds, because we do not have the persistence to plan out and achieve them?

Napoleon Hill, in his book *Think and Grow Rich* said that, "the building of a fortune generally involves the application of the entire thirteen principles of this philosophy. These principles must be understood—all who wish to accumulate money must apply them with *persistence.*" The thirteen factors that were included in this fantastic book are as follows:

- Desire
- Faith
- Autosuggestion
- Specialized Knowledge
- Imagination
- Organized Planning
- Decision
- Persistence
- The Master Mind

- Sex Transmutation
- The Subconscious Mind
- The Brain
- The Sixth Sense

Although all these are listed as factors that contribute to our success, Napoleon Hill asserts that none of these factors is as important as ***persistence***.

Persistence to achieve the goals you set for yourself will be the deciding factor as to whether you create a better financial future for you and your family.

If you have the patience to plan your future, develop faith in your ability to create a better life, and learn the specialised knowledge that you need to invest wisely; if you surround yourself with people who can help you succeed, continue to learn ways to harness the power of your thoughts and emotions—and then apply this knowledge with persistence, then I am one hundred percent sure you will have a better financial future than the one you are presently headed for.

HOW LONG TO A MILLION?

> *"What you get never makes you happy. It's who you become long term that makes you happy or sad"*
>
> —*Anthony Robbins*

Once you realize how quickly the dream of becoming a millionaire can be fulfilled, you will find the inspiration to set this goal for yourself—and the faith and perseverance to make it happen.

Jim Rohn once said that "everyone should have a goal of becoming a millionaire, not for the money, but for the person you will become in the process."

Most people think of a million dollars (or a million pounds) as an amount that is completely outside of their capability to create unless they get lucky and win the lottery. But achieving this milestone isn't as farfetched as you may think. Again, it all comes down to planning: First, planning what it is you want and then committing to a strategy to get you there.

For example, let's say you had just $1,000 to start out with. How long could it take for this $1000 to turn into a *million*?

Well, if you saved it in the bank and earned 5percent interest each year on your money, then it would take 284 years for it to grow to a million. I'm guessing that you may not be around by then!

If you added just $250 per month to your $1,000 at 5percent return, then it would take only 132 years instead of 284 years to reach your goal of a million. Still too long? I thought so.

But, if you took the time and learned just a few strategies for investing this $1,000, what difference might that make?

Well, if you learned an investment strategy that earned you 8percent per month instead of 5percent per year on your $1,000, it would now take you only ten years—that's right, ten years—to turn your $1000 into over a *million*! And that's without adding anything extra to your starting capital!

Alternately, you could take that same $1000 and invest it into a business. If you bought $1,000 worth of products and sold them for $2,000 over the course of the year, and if you reinvested the profits each year to do the same thing, it would still only take you ten years to turn your $1,000 into a *million*.

Does this information inspire you to consider learning some new strategies that will earn you greater returns on your money?

Would it be worth some of the precious time that you have available in order to educate yourself on better ways to make more of your money than you would by putting it in the bank or into a retirement fund? For most, the answer to this question is a resounding "Yes!"

THE MONEY PUZZLE TIME LOG

It's important that you create as much *time* as you can by reducing or eliminating wasted time spent on activities that do not support you. To help you get started, review your activities from last week and complete the time log below.

Add up the minutes you spent doing things that do not help you create the life you want, then consider whether the price you pay for spending your time in this fashion is really worth it.

Use what you learn from this exercise to make more powerful choices regarding your time. For example, if you discovered that you are currently spending three hours a night watching TV, you could decide to invest some or all of that time in learning about alternative investment options.

FOR EACH DAY RECORD IN MINUTES THE NUMBER OF HOURS SPENT AT EACH ACTIVITY								
	MONDAY	TUESDAY	WEDNESDAY	THURSDAY	FRIDAY	SATURDAY	SUNDAY	TOTAL
E MAILS								
Unplanned Telephone Calls								
Reading newspaper								
Idle Chatter								
Shopping								
Meetings								
Watching TV								
Surfing Internet								
Driving/ travelling								
Productive work related activities								
Listening to music								
UnImportant childrens/ spouse activities								
Important chil- drens/spouse activities								
Cooking								
Eating/ drinking								
Sporting activities								
Educational reading								
Study								
SLEEPING								
Other:								
Other:								
Other:								

MONEY PUZZLE MASTERY EXERCISES—TIME

After reading this chapter and seriously thinking about its content, what are the three most important things for you to remember about *time*?

1. _____
2. _____
3. _____

How has learning this affected the way you think about your financial future?

_____

_____

_____

_____

Based on what you learned in this chapter, what actions do you intend to take in order to create a more successful and abundant future?

1. _____
2. _____
3. _____
4. _____
5. _____

6

WHAT'S HOLDING YOU BACK?

> *"Your circumstances may be uncongenial, but they shall not long remain so if you perceive an ideal and strive to reach it"*
>
> —*James Allen*

THE "I CAN'T" SYNDROME

THE "I can't" syndrome destroys more dreams and desires than anything else in life. Not only does this mindset convince you that you will never achieve your goals, but even worse, it can prevent you from daring to dream in the first place.

I once heard a great saying by Henry Ford; "If you say you can or if you say you can't, then either way you are right."

The statement "I can't" actually sets up a belief in your subconscious mind that you will not achieve what it is that you want—before you have even tried! This belief becomes a self-fulfilling prophesy that brings about its own reality.

On the contrary, if you condition your mind to affirm "I can," you are training your mind to look for possibilities, solutions, and resources to help you achieve whatever it is that you want in life.

In his book, *Think and Grow Rich*, Napoleon Hill stated that:

"Whatever the mind can conceive and believe, the mind can achieve"

If you can conceive and believe in your ability to create a financially independent and abundant retirement, this is the first step towards achieving it. Likewise, if you conceive and believe that you can't achieve a financially independent and abundant retirement, it is more than likely that you won't.

Many of us inherited this "I can't" belief from our parents, our teachers, or from society in general. Growing up, we were continually told that we can't do this and we can't do that.

Now, some of this instruction was well-meaning and arose out of our care-givers' desires to keep us safe. However, now that we are adults, we need to question these beliefs by realizing that many of the limiting points of view that were passed on to us are more based on fear than on actual fact. We are the ones who decide for ourselves what is and is not possible. Remember, if you can conceive it, you can achieve it!

> *"Beliefs have the power to create and the power to destroy. Human beings have the awesome ability to take any experience of their lives and create a meaning that disempowers them or one that can literally save their lives"*
>
> —*Anthony Robbins*

SELF-CONFIDENCE AND A WINNER'S IMAGE

Perhaps the most detrimental effect of the "I can't" syndrome is the way it eats away at our self-confidence. Our self-image is the lens through which we see the world. Having high self-confidence and a positive self-image are critical—both for creating success and for enjoying the success we have already achieved.

We base many of our life's decisions on our perceived capabilities—moving ahead on things we feel confident we can achieve and shying away from those we think are beyond our reach. If we hold an image of ourselves failing at some-thing, there is a good chance we won't even try to attain it—even if it's something we really want.

Lack of self-confidence not only prevents us from starting on the road to success, but it can also eat away at the successes we've already achieved. You can probably think of a number of extremely successful people who end up in jail, on drink or drugs, or who have even suffered a premature death, because they lacked the self-confidence and the healthy self-image to back up their success.

On the other hand, if we hold an image of ourselves as being successful and having the ability to achieve what we've set out to do, we tap into inner-strength and outer resources that will help us achieve our goals. Change the way you see yourself, and you will open up to a new world of unlimited opportunities.

Developing self-confidence starts by eliminating the "inner critic"—the part of us that is based on fear and robs us of our motivation and ability to achieve. By focusing on our desires, generating new ideas, and making conscious decisions about what we want from our lives, we can challenge and ultimately eradicate this fear. Once we see that we have the power to assemble plans that will take us in our desired direction, we gain more control over our own destiny.

If you're always telling yourself that you can't achieve something without even attempting to achieve it, how will you ever know if you could or couldn't? One thing is certain: people who don't try fail 100percent of the time. You increase your odds significantly by taking action. By adopting an attitude of "I can," you'll raise your self–confidence, improve your self-image, and have more resources to achieve the results you want in life.

THE BLESSING OF CHALLENGES

Nobody ever said that achieving success would be easy. Yes, you can simplify the process by following the rules and sticking with your plan, but that doesn't guarantee that the journey will be easy.

In fact, easy money can be the most difficult to keep, because you haven't adapted to the idea of having money, and you haven't yet learned how to manage it. This is why a huge percentage of lottery winners end up right back in the same financial situation they were in within five years of winning the lottery.

On the other hand, people who earn their wealth over time have developed the skill set they need to hold onto their money and to keep it growing. This requires a great deal of personal character.

You have to have character to become financially independent. It won't always be smooth sailing, and there will be obstacles and challenges to overcome along the way. But obstacles and challenges are necessary, because they force us to grow, learn, and become more capable in the process.

Becoming successful is all about solving problems. Some people think that those with a lot of money have no problems at all. While it's true that their lives may be more comfortable, I assure you that they still have obstacles and challenges to overcome. Some hurdles will be small and some will be large, but nevertheless we all have them.

Think of the last time you were given a challenge, or an obstacle got in the way of you achieving something. Now, think of how you felt when you overcame that problem. Did your self-confidence go up or down? I'm pretty sure that your confidence went up, no matter how big or small this obstacle was at the time. Now, think of how you would feel if this challenge came up again. Chances are you would feel more confident in your ability to face it, having already conquered it once before.

Most people veer off the path of achieving financial success before they even hit the first hurdle. Even the ones who start are likely to run straight back into their comfort zone at the sight of the first challenge. But the ones who take on the challenge and overcome the obstacles will learn so much about themselves in the process, and this knowledge will propel them on to creating even more success in other areas of their lives.

The Grand National is a horse race of epic proportions in the U.K. All of the contenders set out at the starting line with the goal of reaching the winning post first and winning the race. How much of a chance does a jockey who refuses to jump any hurdles stand of winning? The answer is, not much of a chance at all. The winner of the race will have to jump every single hurdle that comes his way—both small hurdles like the Foinavon Fence, and big daunting hurdles like Beecher's Brook.

The winner will also have to overcome the challenges of racing against his competitors, being bumped around, and having other horses get in the way. He may even face the obstacle of a horse that's lost its rider, running around like a loose cannon and distracting him from the finish line.

You can think about your race toward financial independence as being a bit like the Grand National. All you have to do is get on the starting line, summon the inner resources to face obstacles and challenges in a positive way, and you will surely win the big prize.

The more problems we learn to deal with and the more problems we help others deal with, the more chance of success we have. And the more successful we become, the more skills and experience we will have at our disposal to deal with future problems as they arise.

As we've seen, the current system of retirement provision is a major issue that threatens our financial futures. To overcome this obstacle, we have to start asking ourselves what consequences we are likely to face if we don't create a plan now for our own financial well-being.

Make a decision to become financially independent now. Learn and grow through the obstacles and challenges you will face on the way. Otherwise, you may find that the biggest and toughest hurdle of all will face you later in life, when you don't have enough money and time to solve it in the way you would like.

Jim Rohn also said:

"There are two pains—the pain of discipline and the pain of regret. The pain of discipline weighs ounces, whereas the pain of regret weighs tons."

The pain of discipline is like the short-term pain of sticking with your plan to become financially independent. The pain of regret is like the long-term pain of getting to retirement and running out of money.

ARE YOUR BELIEFS ABOUT MONEY SERVING YOU?

Beliefs are nothing more than a set of specific neural pathways that are programmed into our brains. They are a collection of thought patterns that have been hardwired into our nervous system by repetitively thinking the same thoughts and cultivating the same attitudes.

The problem is that beliefs are not always true.

In fact, some of the strongest beliefs that have ever been held throughout history have been utterly untrue. It wasn't so long ago that people thought the world was flat. This repetitive cluster of thought patterns was so widely held that anyone who disputed the flatness of the world was thought to be quite insane—even punished by death. We also used to believe that the Sun orbited the Earth—again, totally untrue. Both beliefs were based on insufficient knowledge at the time, but they remained strong nonetheless.

We used to believe that man could not run a mile in under four minutes. When Roger Bannister changed that belief within himself, he changed it within the entire world. In the year following Roger Bannister's feat of running the first four-minute mile, dozens of other people also accomplished this, and thousands of people have done so since. What happened? People changed their beliefs because they realized their old beliefs were false.

Money, success, and self are the three major areas in which people hold their most limiting beliefs. If you can identify the limiting beliefs that are holding you back from achieving real financial success, you can turn them into more positive beliefs that will propel you to the success you desire.

What beliefs do you hold about money, success, and yourself? How do you see the world around you and your prospects for creating financial abundance?

Are these beliefs true or false?

Where did these beliefs come from?

Use the worksheet below to begin to expose and challenge the beliefs that may be holding you back.

What do I believe about *money?*	Is this true or false?	Where did this belief come from?
1.		
2.		
3.		
4.		
5.		
6.		
7.		
8.		
9.		
10.		
What do I believe about *success?*	Is this true or false?	Where did this belief come from?
1.		
2.		
3.		
4.		
5.		
6.		
7.		
8.		
9.		
10.		

What do I believe about *myself*?	Is this true or false?	Where did this belief come from?
1.		
2.		
3.		
4.		
5.		
6.		
7.		
8.		
9.		
10.		
What do I believe about *the world around me*?	Is this true or false?	Where did this belief come from?
1.		
2.		
3.		
4.		
5.		
6.		
7.		
8.		
9.		
10.		

What do I believe about *my prospects for creating financial abundance in my life?*	Is this true or false?	Where did this belief come from?
1.		
2.		
3.		
4.		
5.		
6.		
7.		
8.		
9.		
10.		

Have you ever even challenged your habits of thought, opinion, and attitude to determine whether they are true or false?

Henry Ford's saying of "whether you think you can or you think you can't, either way you are right" gets right to the crux of how our beliefs about ourselves produce our external results.

The challenge is to figure out why we think we can't do something, and to uncover what influences have led us to this faulty conclusion. Once we establish what we believe, we can then challenge why we have come to believe it.

More often than not, we will find that our beliefs are nothing more than a collection of thoughts, opinions, and attitudes that have been passed down to us from an early age by family, friends, teachers, and the media. In other words, our beliefs are only there because someone else put them there!

Recognizing the origin of our beliefs puts us right back in the driver's seat to regain control and hardwire some new, more empowering beliefs into our brains—beliefs that will support us in achieving the specific goals we have set for ourselves.

Do you know that 96percent to 98percent of all our behaviors are automatic? Consequently, we can set about developing new inspiring thoughts and attitudes that our subconscious minds can use to create new behaviors and actions that will transform our lives.

Most of what we think comes down to the beliefs we hold. Limiting beliefs in any area of our lives will affect the way we think, which will in turn affect the actions we take, and ultimately the results we create. The results we create then reinforce the previously held limiting belief and strengthen it even further.

This will go on like a continually revolving thought process unless we do something to break the circuit. One way to break the circuit is to change the results we produce, but in order to change our results, we need to change the actions we take. We could change the actions we take, but these actions are based on how we think. We could just change the way we think, but how can we possibly do that unless we change the beliefs we hold about the area we want to improve?

The good news is that the cycle can work just as perfectly on the positive side of things as it does on the negative. If we have positive beliefs about things, this will result in more positive thinking about that area. The positive thinking will result in better quality actions, which will in turn lead to better results, which will again reinforce the positive beliefs that we hold, and possibly make them stronger.

Change your negative beliefs to more positive ones and you'll see a better result. It was Buddha who said:

"All that we are is the result of what we have thought."

If all that we think is based upon what we believe, then what we believe will create our outcomes.

This further supports my earlier explanation of the "I can't" syndrome. If we believe we can't, we won't. But if we believe we can, we will!

THE "WHAT WILL PEOPLE THINK?" SYNDROME

"What will people think?" is a question many people ask themselves continually, even over the most basic of life situations.

The "What will people think?" syndrome stems from the idea that we should be doing what everyone else is doing; that we must follow the crowd in order to be accepted. I heard a great quote that said

"If you see a huge crowd going one way down a street and only a few people going the other way, then follow the few and you won't go far wrong." - *Anonymous*

It comes back to the beliefs we hold about ourselves, our self-images and the attachments we have to material things such as money, houses, cars, and vacations. Many people believe that if they don't collect the same toys as everyone else, or if they do not achieve what they set out to achieve, then somehow people will see them differently.

The reverse is also true. I think a lot of people believe that if they achieve massive financial success, people will treat them differently. This kind of thinking keeps people stuck doing the same things as their friends, families, and peers, because they don't want to be seen as *different*. What is more important? You and your financial security or what your friends think?

Yes, money will change things in your life. It will make you more comfortable, but it does not have to change the person you really are. In fact, having more money and more success will enhance the person you already are. So, if you are a kind, genuine person who considers the needs of others and thinks positively on a daily basis, having more money will just enhance those qualities.

Conversely, if you are a negative-thinking, selfish, greedy, rude, or unkind person, having more money will enhance these features of your personality as well. You'll become even more rude and unkind, even more greedy and selfish, and think even more negative thoughts every day.

FOLLOWING THE CROWD IS A DANGEROUS PLAN

If you are currently saving into a company retirement fund, a personal retirement fund or a pooled investment in the stock market, you may be following financial advice that is decades old.

If you took ten minutes to really think about the reason you are pursuing this course of action for your retirement, you would likely discover that you're doing it not because you considered it deeply and found it to be the most effective course of action, but because you are adhering to the status quo or following someone else's plan.

The question you have to ask yourself is, "Will following someone else's plan produce the outcome I want in life?"

To plan a financially abundant future, you have to separate important facts from irrelevant information. Once you are able to do this you will be able to think clearly and accurately about where you are really headed with regard to your finances.

Facts that enhance or expedite the attainment of your financial goals are important and relevant; but of course, in order to recognize them when you come across them, you must first know what your goals are.

Napoleon Hill, in his book *The Law of Success* said:

"… that you may understand the importance of distinguishing between facts and mere information, study the type of man who is guided entirely by that of which he hears; the type that is influenced by all the 'whisperings of the winds of gossip'; that accepts, without analysis, all that he reads in the newspapers."

With so much conflicting information coming at us from all sources, it's more important than ever to take the time to analyze and fully understand what we read and what we hear.

Only when you are intimately familiar with the details of your own financial situation can you knowingly and consciously make a positive impact in your financial future.

Before continuing on your current plan for retirement, I urge you to stop and give some real consideration to the options and choices that are available to help you plan for your future. Then you can implement a course of action that is based upon your needs and desires rather than following someone else's plan and ending up with a life that is not of your making.

MONEY CONDITIONING

Let's review the beliefs about money that you listed earlier. As you look at all the limiting or negative beliefs that you wrote down, notice how many of them are the result of the conditioning about money that you learned as you were growing up. I'm going to suggest that many of the beliefs you currently hold about money were instilled in you by your parents, grandparents, teachers, or other authority figures that influenced you early in life. But from where did your parents, grandparents, teachers, and other leaders get their beliefs from? That's right, from their parents, grandparents, teachers, and other authority figures that had an influence on them.-

As you got a little older, you were then exposed to newspapers, television, and other media that further guided your beliefs about money. You were also influenced by your friends and their parents and the beliefs and attitudes they held about money.

So, in actuality, the beliefs that govern your actions today were instilled into you decades ago. Is it any wonder then, why you do things with money that make no sense in your life today? The fact is that the beliefs your parents and grandparents held were from a totally different financial paradigm, and may not necessarily be of any benefit to you today.

As compared to your parents and grandparents, you live in a world where there is an abundance of opportunity to become financially successful, and you also live in a world where anyone can communicate and do business on a global scale.

In addition, you are living in the information age; whereas your grandparents lived in the industrial age. And yet, most of the financial advice you receive is still based on what was appropriate during the industrial age!

Unless you make a conscious effort to override them, these antiquated beliefs about money and financial planning may keep you from becoming wealthy, and could actually cause you to become poorer in your retirement.

DON'T LET YOUR LIMITATIONS HOLD YOU BACK

> *"Belief in limitation is the one and only thing that causes limitation; because we thus impress limitation upon the creative principle; and in proportion as we lay that belief aside our boundaries will expand, and increasing life and more abundant blessing will be ours"*
>
> —*Thomas Troward*

Each one of us has a different definition of what it means to be financially secure. And, depending on our starting points, it may take some of us longer than others to reach our financial goals. But, the fact is that everyone has the ability to make a success of their lives; they need only to apply their assets and skills to make it happen.

You could look at anyone's situation, whether they have severe physical limitations or severe financial limitations, and find someone with the same—if not identical—conditions, who has become successful in life.

Anthony Robbins once shared a story about a man named Ed Roberts to illustrate why personal challenges are no excuse for why we can't make more of our lives and create a better world others as well. Before he died in 1995, Ed Roberts spent nearly half his life in an iron lung and the other half in a wheelchair. However, he became the first quadriplegic to graduate from the University of California, served as director of the California State Department of Rehabilitation, and became one of the founders and champions of the disability rights movement.

There are more opportunities today to achieve financial success than ever before. In fact, sometimes I think there are so many opportunities that we often find it difficult to choose the right one at any given time.

Of course, someone who has $100,000 in the bank, has no children, owns his home outright, and has a successful business will obviously have a head start on someone who rents his home, has three children, owes $30,000 on credit cards and loans, and works for someone else.

However, both of these people still have unlimited potential to achieve whatever they desire in life as long as they set their goals, decide what they want, set a plan for achieving a specific goal, and stick with the plan until the goal is achieved.

The point is—it doesn't matter what constraints you are currently dealing with, you can still achieve a financially independent future and realize your unlimited potential—you just need the right plan in place to help you succeed.

THE "IF ONLY" SYNDROME

The "if only" syndrome is a killer of financial success, as it gives you a perfect excuse or alibi as to why you can't be bothered to sit down and think through the innumerable ways that you could achieve any goal you set for yourself.

The "if only" excuses that you've created and habitually defend are really only a smokescreen for the real reasons you aren't working a plan towards financial independence. When held long enough, these excuses keep us stuck in the status quo and resigned to the belief that this is "just how things are."

In his book, *Think and Grow Rich*, Napoleon Hill gave the following fifty-four commonly used "if only" excuses used at the time to explain away failure and lack of achievement. This book was written in 1937, but I wonder how many of these excuses are still being used today to justify the lack of financial success, even though today we have far more opportunities to create an abundance of wealth and retire young and rich than most people had back in 1937.

Just take a look at the list and see if any of these excuses have stopped you from building a brighter financial future for you and your family:

1. If only I didn't have a wife and family
2. If only I had enough "pull" (authority)
3. If only I had money
4. If only I had a good education
5. If only I could get a job
6. If only I had good health
7. If only I had time
8. If only times were better
9. If only other people understood me
10. If only conditions around me were different
11. If only I could live my life over again
12. If only I did not fear what *they* would say
13. If only I had been given a chance
14. If only I now had a chance
15. If only other people didn't have it in for me
16. If only nothing happens to stop me
17. If only I were younger
18. If only I could do what I want
19. If only I had been born rich
20. If only I could meet the right people
21. If only I had the talent that some people had
22. If only I dared assert myself
23. If only I had embraced past opportunities
24. If only people didn't get on my nerves
25. If only I didn't have to keep house and look after the children
26. If only I could save some money
27. If only the boss appreciated me
28. If only I had someone to help me
29. If only my family understood me

30. If only I lived in a big city
31. If only I could just get started
32. If only I were free
33. If only I had the personality of some people
34. If only I were not so fat
35. If only my talents were known
36. If only I could just get a break
37. If only I could get out of debt
38. If only I hadn't failed
39. If only I knew how
40. If only everybody didn't oppose me
41. If only I didn't have so many worries
42. If only I could marry the right person
43. If only people weren't so dumb
44. If only my family weren't so extravagant
45. If only I was sure of myself
46. If only luck were not against me
47. If only I hadn't been born under the wrong star
48. If only it were not true that "what is to be will be"
49. If only I didn't have to work so hard
50. If only I hadn't lost my money
51. If only I lived in a different neighbourhood
52. If only I didn't have a "past"
53. If only I had a business of my own
54. If only other people would listen to me

When it comes to planning a wealthy future there is only one person that is going to be able to do this for you and that is—*you*!

So, unless you conquer yourself and stop making excuses as to why you can't achieve any level of financial success you set out to achieve, you will remain bound and gagged by these alibis for the rest of your life.

The only way you will ever break through the shackles of the excuses you are using—whether consciously or unconsciously—is to envision the life you want to create and then set about making it happen. Everything else you can learn on the way.

To finish off his list of "if only" excuses, Napoleon Hill then shared what he considered to be "greatest *if only* of them all":

"If only I had the courage to see myself as I really am, I would find out what is wrong with me, and correct it, then I might have a chance to profit by my mistakes and learn something from the experience of others, for I know that there is something *wrong* with me, or I would now be where I *would have been if* I had spent more time analyzing my weaknesses, and less time building alibis to cover them."

WOW!

Now, if we take this statement and use it to look at our financial planning, especially when it comes to planning for retirement, we can see that instead of using excuses to explain away why we haven't taken more responsibility for our finances in the past, we could summon the courage to see things for how they really are. We could find out what's wrong, correct it by taking better action, learn from our mistakes, learn from others' experiences by continuing to educate ourselves, and spend less time believing the excuses that have prevented us from being more financially secure than we already are.

DON'T QUIT ON YOUR DREAMS

Most people quit on their dreams and desires far too soon and revert to settling for "what is." When we were children, we always dreamed big dreams and wanted to become things like an astronaut, a princess, a king, a rock star, or a professional athlete. We thought we could do anything we wanted to.

Why then, as soon as we leave school and enter adulthood, do we just settle for "what is"? Do we feel we are victims, and that we just have to accept what is dealt to us? Do we just want an easy life and cannot be bothered to think of other ways that we could achieve more? Are we just too lazy to sit down and start planning a more successful future? Or, does our laziness arise because we have lost the faith that we can, in fact, make a difference?

And then, even if we sit down and set goals for our lives and design a plan for achieving them, we still stop and revert to "what is" as soon as we hit an obstacle or hurdle.

"A QUITTER NEVER WINS AND A WINNER NEVER QUITS"

It is a certain fact that you will never attain any dream if you do not dream it to begin with. You will never attain your dream if you do not act to achieve it, and it's absolutely certain you will never attain your dream if you give up too soon and settle for "what is."

I once heard a great story, called "Three Feet from Gold," that explains why you should never, ever give up on your dream, because you really don't know how close you are to achieving it. It is about a man who was caught by gold fever in the gold rush days. He went west to dig and grow rich, and after a few weeks of hard work, he was rewarded by the discovery of some shining ore. He went back home to tell his friends and family about his find, and they all got together the money to purchase the machinery that was needed to bring the ore to the surface. When they mined the first ore, they found that they had one of the richest mines in Colorado. So, down went the drills and up went their hopes of the richness they were going to reap. Then, all of a sudden, the vein of ore disappeared. They drilled on, desperately trying to pick up the vein again, but with no success. They decided to quit on their dream. They sold the machinery to a junk man for a few hundred dollars and went back home. The junk man called in a mining engineer and, with a little calculating, the engineer advised that the project had failed because the owners were not familiar with fault lines. His calculations showed that the vein would be found just *three feet* from where the others had stopped drilling. That is exactly where it was, and the junk man became rich.

How often do we stop just three feet from gold in pursuit of our dreams just because we are faced with a challenge or an obstacle? In these times it may seem the easiest thing—even the most logical thing—to quit on your dream. Sadly, this is what the majority of people do. This is why it is so critical to create your goals and dreams with a compelling vision, and be fully aware of the big reasons why you want to achieve them. It is in the vision and the reason why that your resolve can stand up to the challenges and temporary defeats that you will surely meet on your path to success.

Napoleon Hill said, "more than 500 of the most successful people America has ever known reported that their greatest success came just one step beyond the point at which defeat had overtaken them. Failure is a trickster with a keen sense of irony and cunning. It takes great delight in tripping one up when success is almost within reach." Please, make sure this does not happen to you!

WHAT'S THE WORST THAT COULD HAPPEN?

When we fear doing something new—especially when it comes to investing—we often paint pictures in our minds of all the bad things that could happen, and all the things that could go wrong.

> *"Named must your fear be before banish it you can"*
> —*Yoda*

When stacked upon each other, all these negative pictures swirl round and round in loops in our minds, eventually stopping us from taking the necessary actions to become financially successful.

Most people are fearful of doing something different because they don't know where to start. They don't have the knowledge, so they think endlessly about the things that could go wrong.

The best question that you could ask in this case is:

"What is the worst that could happen if I learn more about this by taking action and trying something new?"

It is best to actually write your answers to this question down, because it gets the thoughts out of your mind and onto paper.

Quite often, what seems like an endless list of things that could go wrong, turn out to be only a few, but because they are locked away in your mind where they compound and multiply, you get the impression that there are far more things that could go wrong than actually could.

Once you've written all of the things that could possibly go wrong on the left side of the page, there are a few things you can do to dispel the risks, challenge the likelihood that they will happen, and help prevent them from happening. On the right side of the page, ask yourself the following questions:

"How likely is it that this could really happen?"

"What would I do next if this event did happen?"

We often get it into our heads that if something bad should happen, it would simply be the end of us; we would be complete failures, and we would find no way to redeem ourselves. By getting irrational thoughts like these out of your head and onto paper, you will realize that there are always solutions to any scenario, and that even if the worst did occur, it would not be the end of the world, and there would always be a way back.

One of the biggest things that could go wrong today is doing nothing and continuing on a financial path that is just not working. So, we could even turn this question around and use it to ask:

"What is the worst that could happen if I keep doing what I'm currently doing?"

You will soon see that financial failure is far more likely to occur by following the same path, than it is by doing something different and taking control of your own financial destiny. By leaving it until you actually retire to find out if you have built up enough money to provide the income you need, you run the risk of not being able to recover from this worst-case scenario. You would be left wondering for the rest of your life what could have been, had you only taken the risk earlier on in life and dealt with the challenges on the way.

THE NO LIMIT ATTITUDE OF CHILDREN

Children can teach adults a lot about freedom and going after what they want. They are persistent, they have a "no limits" attitude when it comes to their wishes and desires, and they go about getting what they want with complete and utter enthusiasm.

It's only when we adults persuade them otherwise by saying things like, "You can't always have what you want." and "Who do you think you are?" and "Do you think that money grows on trees?" that they start giving up on their hopes and dreams and resign themselves to the status quo—even if it doesn't fulfil their desires.

We are born without limits. As babies, we come into this world as a blank canvass with the potential to do and become whatever we want. It's only when we start taking on the attitudes and behaviors of our parents, grandparents, teachers, and other influencers in our lives that this potential is suffocated, and we enter into a world of lack and limitation; of accepting "what is." When this happens, our "no limits" attitude is replaced by the feeling that we can't do any better, and our enthusiasm is replaced by complacency.

Just watch a young child at play, and you'll see an enthusiasm for life that we all started out with. That enthusiasm for life enables them to do whatever it is they want without fear and without limitation.

Maybe our children could teach us all a thing or two about what we could be capable of in our lives if we allowed ourselves to really go for what we want.

THE WORRY OF FAILURE

The worry of failure breeds inaction. This in turn leads to failure, or worse, following a course that someone else has planned for you in life.

Plato once said that:

"The first and best victory is to conquer self. To be conquered by self is, of all things, the most shameful and vile."

Just take a look at the following passage from *Think and Grow Rich* by Napoleon Hill and see that the worry of failure is an obstacle that must be overcome in one's own mind. By conquering this fear, and therefore conquering ourselves, we are propelled toward brighter financial futures than we could ever imagine.

"Worry is a state of mind based upon fear. It works slowly, but persistently. It is insidious and subtle. Step by step it digs itself in until it paralyses one's reasoning faculty and destroys self confidence and initiative. Worry is a form of sustained fear caused by indecision. Therefore it is a state of mind which can be controlled. Kill the habit of worry, in all its forms, by reaching a general, blanket decision that nothing that life has to offer is worth the price of worry. With this decision will come poise, peace of mind and calmness of thought that will bring you happiness. A man whose mind is filled with fear destroys his own chances of intelligent action."

Education is the key to mastering fear and worry. By educating ourselves about the trends and threats to future financial security and by educating ourselves about available alternatives to build greater security, we will rid ourselves of the fear of failure forever.

THE SHACKLES OF FEAR

Fear is by far the biggest shackle to shake off when you are starting out on the path to financial freedom. By definition, becoming financially independent requires you to do some things you have never done before, so it's only natural to feel a bit anxious. That doesn't mean you need to permit fear to stop you in your tracks.

When presented with a new idea or plan that challenges a familiar way of doing things, most people let fear take hold of them. They go straight back to their old way of life because it feels safe—even though the old way of doing things is probably the thing to fear most.

Another thing that causes people to fear change is the notion of doing something different from what the majority of people around them are doing. Our past conditioning tells us that there is safety in numbers, so we often follow the lead set by the majority of people.

But the majority of people still don't know what you've already learned about retirement. They don't yet understand how vital it is to take control of their own financial destinies. In this respect, you are ahead of the crowd. It might seem scary right now, but I assure you, taking charge of your financial future now will offer you far more security than continuing to bury your head in the sand.

In our journey to financial freedom, fear is the number one obstacle that must be challenged and overcome. Just because something is new does not mean it should be feared or avoided. You can learn as you go, just like you did when you learned to ride a bike, drive a car, write a report, or raise a child.

A frequently used acronym for fear is *False Evidence Appearing Real.* When it comes to investing money to build assets for the future, this definition is particularly descriptive. When considering new strategies to employ with their money, people often paint the pictures of loss and failure in their mind as if they are already a reality. The false evidence they've imagined appears real, so they go back to where they feel safest, doing what they are doing now.

However, doing what we do now only brings more of what we are getting. If we expect different results from taking the same actions, then maybe it's time for a visit to the doctor, as this is verging on insanity!

Take a real hard look at the path you are on now with regard to your retirement planning and your finances. What's more frightening: taking a risk to do something different or continuing down the same path you're on? If you're honest, you may find that maintaining the status quo is really the thing you should fear.

In *Think and Grow Rich*, Napoleon Hill describes what he calls the "Ghosts of Fear." Here are three of them:

- The Fear of Poverty
- The Fear of Criticism
- The Fear of Old Age

Unless they are confronted and overcome, these fears will continue to hold you back from doing something new, and can seriously sabotage your goal to become financially independent. Let's dismantle them one by one.

The Fear of Criticism is born out of our desire to follow the crowd and our reluctance to try something new. This fear robs us of initiative, imagination, and self-reliance to create the lives of our dreams. *The Fear of Old Age* is intimately linked to *The Fear of Poverty,* as most people's perception of retirement is of a poorer standard of living and of failing health. *The Fear of Poverty* can be overcome by refusing to accept any circumstance regarding poverty and thinking only in terms of creating the financial independence you deserve.

You've already come so far! You've decided what it is you want. You've created a compelling vision of a prosperous and financially free retirement. You've figured out how much money you will need and when you will need it. But if you neglect to start, or stop before you arrive, chances are that you are in the grips of fear.

Fear is nothing more than a state of mind, and yet the indifference, indecision, doubt, worry, over-caution, and procrastination it creates are powerful enough to kill any off dream and/or desire.

However, fear can only destroy our dreams if we insist on focusing on the things that could potentially go wrong. Most of our fears exist only within our own minds rather than in the reality of the situation. It's the negative "what if's" that go round and round in endless loops inside our heads, creating a fear that if you do take action toward your dreams and desires, something will go wrong and you'll lose everything.

This thinking just strips away the self-confidence you need to set and attain any goal that you want in life. Yes, things can go wrong, and yes, things don't always go exactly the way you planned. But what does go wrong and what doesn't go perfectly is never, in reality, as bad as the fear that swims through the minds of most people and prevents them from taking action.

In Brian Tracy's book, *Flight Plan*, he shares a startling fact: every plane flying en route toward a particular destination is off course on its journey 99 percent of the time. That means that for 99percent of the time it is correcting its course of action in order to arrive at its appointed destination. Every pilot knows this, yet does this fact prevent him from taking off? Does the prospect of turbulence or updrafts, crosswinds, storms, or lightning prevent the pilot from taking off toward his destination? No, of course not.

A good pilot knows there are risks and is well aware of the things that could go wrong. He knows that he will be off course for 99percent of the journey. However, he does not let the cloud of fear overtake him and keep him stuck on the runway. He rises above these fears in order to deliver himself and others to the desired destination.

The same is true for planning ahead financially. The moment we create a dream, a goal or desire to be more, have more, or do more with our lives, we will confront the very fears that have kept us living a life of mediocrity instead of excellence. We would love to quit our jobs and start businesses, or invest money in ways that could create exponential growth, but the fear that crosswinds, turbulence, and storms may occur takes over—paralyzing us in our tracks.

Too often, the fear of what we could lose keeps us from taking any action at all. We go back to doing what we have always done, and relinquish control over our financial futures. Although it feels as if we are running for cover, failing to move forward on our financial goals is probably the most risky course of action that we could take.

The only way to overcome fear is by taking action. By thinking accurately and clearly about where our lives are headed, and by taking actions that demonstrate that we are responsible for our own financial futures, we expose fear for what it really is: False Evidence Appearing Real.

MONEY PUZZLE MASTERY EXERCISES—
WHAT'S HOLDING YOU BACK?

After reading this chapter and seriously thinking about its content, what are the three most important things that need to remember about *what is holding you back from achieving what you want in life?*

1. _____
2. _____
3. _____

How has learning this affected the way you think about your financial future?

_____
_____
_____
_____

Based on what you have learned in this chapter, what actions do you intend to take in order to create a more successful and abundant future?

1. _____
2. _____
3. _____
4. _____
5. _____
6. _____

Remember and write down a time when you said "I can't" to something:

_____

_____

_____

_____

Remember and write down a time when you said "I can" to something:

_____

_____

_____

_____

What was the difference in your feelings and the outcomes you achieved?

_____

_____

_____

_____

What are your thoughts and feelings on becoming wealthy?

_____

_____

_____

_____

What challenges and obstacles have you already overcome in your life?

_____

_____

_____

_____

How did you overcome them? What steps did you take?

_____

_____

_____

_____

Are your beliefs about money, success, retirement, yourself, and your abilities empowering you or disempowering you?

_____

_____

_____

_____

What are your views about risk?

_____

_____

_____

_____

Have you ever been out of your comfort zone?

_____

_____

_____

_____

What did it feel like?

_____

_____

_____

_____

What did you do when you were outside your comfort zone?

_____

_____

_____

_____

What kind of person do you think you will become if you have a huge amount of money?

_____

_____

_____

_____

What qualities would having a lot of money enhance in you?

_____

_____

_____

_____

Why are you following your current plan for your retirement?

_____

_____

_____

_____

How likely is it that this plan will produce the outcome you want?

_____

_____

_____

_____

What excuses or alibis have you used in the past for not becoming financially independent yet?

_____
_____
_____
_____

Have you ever quit too soon on something you wanted? Why? How did you feel?

_____
_____
_____
_____

What are your major financial concerns right now?

_____
_____
_____
_____

7

RISK

> *"Risk comes from not knowing what you're doing"*
>
> —*Warren Buffet*

THE MISCONCEPTION OF RISK

RISK is widely misunderstood in our society, especially when it comes to finances. Most people think that in order to become wealthy you have to take risks. This is perfectly true. The problem is that the illusionary fear of risk holds most people back from even assessing the risks they'll need to take to create real wealth. And people also tend to ignore the risks they are actually taking by pursuing their current courses of action.

The biggest financial risk for people today is doing nothing and staying with the same financial plan they've had in the past. As you've learned already, the world has changed. Refusing to change along with it is a risk that none of us can afford to take.

> *"You are the only problem you will ever have and you are the only solution. Change is inevitable, personal growth is always a personal decision"*
>
> —*Bob Proctor*

Some of our misconceptions about risk arise because we associate risk with the need to change our ways, and change takes us out of our comfort zones. Outside of our comfort zones we feel threatened, even though the actual threat or risk may not be that big.

Most people's view of risk—especially with regard to money and investing—

has been passed down from previous generations where scarcity was the norm. Our grandparents and great grandparents lived through the Great Depression of the 1930s, two world wars, and the strict rationing of resources that was the norm during that period. Furthermore, they lived in an era where most people were looked after by their company or government—a luxury that our generation can no longer rely upon.

Understanding the risks involved with continuing on the current course of action—and learning what other options are available to us—are essential if we wish to build a more secure financial future.

In today's economy, the financial strategies to which we are accustomed—such as paying off a home as soon as possible, saving for a rainy day, and putting money in a retirement fund—could actually become a massive liability later on in life. On the other hand, by taking the risk to step out of our comfort zones and follow a new path to financial freedom, we actually gain more personal control over our destinies and can look forward to a more comfortable lifestyle later on in life.

UNDERSTANDING WHAT RISK REALLY IS

To overcome the financial fears that have plagued us in the past, we have to understand what risk really is. When it comes to investing, most people define risk as gambling with their money. This understanding, of course, breeds the fear of loss, which in turn stops them from taking action, and they remain more or less making the same choices with their money year after year.

The real definition of risk is doing something that you haven't done before with the intention of mastering the feeling of uncertainty that comes with it, so you become more and more comfortable each time you step outside your familiar comfort zone.

It's also important to understand that not every risk is a high risk. Warren Buffet has never gone into any investment without an element of risk; Donald Trump has never invested in any property without any risk; and Richard Branson has never invested in any business without taking a risk. People who have solved the money puzzle know that risk is simply part of the equation; the difference is that they take *calculated risks*. They weigh up the potential benefits of a given deal against all the things that could go wrong. Then they build contingencies into their plans to hedge against the potential risks. Rarely do they move forward with a deal unless the odds are stacked more in favor of a positive outcome than a negative outcome.

As I mentioned earlier, when you fly in an airplane headed for any destination, you will be off course 99percent of the time. Yes, there is risk in taking off, and yes, there is risk along the way, and yes, there is risk in landing at the destination! But by staying where you are, you run the risk of being left on the runway of your own life while the world moves on around you.

There is a wonderful poem in Bob Proctor's book *You Were Born Rich* that speaks directly to this point:

> To laugh is to risk appearing the fool.
> To weep is to risk appearing sentimental.
> To reach out for another is to risk involvement.
> To expose feelings for another is to risk exposing your true self.
> To place your ideas, your dreams, before a crowd is to risk their loss.
> To love is to risk not being loved in return.
> To live is to risk dying.
> To hope is to risk despair.
> To try is to risk failure.

You may avoid suffering and sorrow if you don't risk, but you will never learn, feel, change, grow, love, or live without it. The greatest hazard in life is to risk nothing. The person who risks nothing, does nothing, and has nothing. Only a person who risks is truly free.

WITHOUT RISK, WE CANNOT LEARN

How do we learn?

Basically, we learn by trying something we haven't tried before, by failing, adapting, trying again, failing, adapting, trying again. We correct our actions based upon what we've learned—both as a result of the things that have gone well and the things that haven't gone so well.

I recently heard a great phrase that describes this process: "Failing Upwards."

Just think how many new skills we learned when we were children. Walking, running, climbing, falling, talking, eating, tying our shoelaces—did we ever just try these new things and—hey, presto!— find that we could do them immediately?

No, we learned to do these things by doing them, failing, adapting, and doing them again and again until they were second nature. This is what's called "failing upwards."

Just yesterday I was teaching my eight-year-old son how to tie his shoelaces. At first he was all fingers and thumbs; he didn't have a clue where to put the laces and couldn't coordinate his movements well enough to get the laces tied. He was very frustrated at first, as he tried and failed and tried and failed again. However, after a few times of trying, failing, learning, and adapting, he did it. You should have seen the look on his face when finally he succeeded and tied his own laces for the first time.

So why, when we become adults do we keep ourselves locked in imaginary prisons of doing nothing new because it seems risky when, throughout our whole childhood, we learned by doing the complete opposite?

It's essential to take risks. It is the only way we build the confidence to know that we have what it takes to overcome life's challenges. With knowledge and experience we can become adept at anything we put our minds to.

THE BIGGEST RISK—DOING NOTHING AT ALL

The risk of doing nothing is the biggest risk of all. Even though it may feel safe to keep doing the same things with your money, by planning your financial future with the same strategies you used to plan your past, you may be following a path that will leave you short of the resources you'll need in retirement—and also short of time to correct your course. Millions of people are taking the risk of running out of money later in life, and only by incorporating new habits with their money can they hope to change this most certain of scenarios.

Imagine being in a row boat gently gliding along the Niagara River. You could row for miles and miles quite easily with no concerns, and everything would seem safe. Now imagine that somebody came along and told you that you really should not go too much farther down this river in just a row boat—otherwise you will run out of time and find yourself tumbling over one of the biggest waterfalls in the world. They suggest that you either turn around immediately, or change the vehicle in which you are travelling to a more high-powered boat that you can turn around and get out of danger quickly, should the need arise. But because you feel safe in your old row boat, and because it is what you have been doing up until now, you decide to ignore the advice and keep going using the same vehicle that you've been travelling in for years.

At some point, you will see the falls in the distance, but unfortunately, by then it will be too late to make a new choice, and you will be sucked over the falls to almost certain death.

The time to change your habits and course of action is not when you are in clear sight of danger, but when things feel safe. This is why the biggest risk of all is to keep doing what you've always done and not take the risk of changing your course of action. Think of the traditional forms of financial planning like the Niagara River. Think of your own financial habits as your row boat. Think of Niagara Falls as your retirement date.

And think of your new high-powered boat as the financial plan that you could put in place right now; a plan that has the power to steer you away from danger before it appears and guarantees you a truly secure retirement.

THE RISKIEST ADVICE IS MOST OFTEN THE CHEAPEST

When it comes to your finances, the riskiest advice you can receive is, more often than not, the cheapest advice around. I'm speaking here of the free advice and the opinions of family, friends, and colleagues who often know no different, and do not even understand the advice they are giving.

Another big risk is taking advice from newspaper reports that exist purely to sell papers and captivate readers' attention by using fear-based headlines that shock people into buying the paper.

Believing inaccurate or biased information as opposed to understanding what is really happening in the financial world can make a big difference in your own financial future.

It all comes down to *educating* yourself effectively about the financial world, money, retirement, asset creation, stock markets, property, and business— and this education does not come free.

The best investment you can make is in your own education. By following sound advice from expert sources, you ensure that the decisions you are making on your own behalf are based on accurate information.

OVERCOMING RISKS

Thinking about how we learned to drive is a powerful way of understanding how we overcome risks because it helps us to realize that once we learn how to do something, the risks become smaller. Overcoming risk and fear requires conscious effort—the same as learning to drive required conscious effort—until you learned how to do it, and it became automatic.

Think back to when you first learned to drive. I'm willing to bet that it was pretty scary, and the risks of crashing were very high, because you didn't know how and when to do all the things that you needed to do. You also had to concentrate on all of the other drivers on the road, the signs, lights, diversions, crossings, and other people. It was difficult enough to get the pedals pushed down in the correct sequence so that the car wouldn't stall, and to keep the steering steady enough so that you weren't all over the road—let alone checking your mirror, indicating your turn signals, and looking at the road ahead for danger. But, soon enough—after going through the process of learning, doing, adapting, and repeating—the whole process became automatic. Not only were you able to drive the car effectively without much thought of the risk of crashing, but you were now able to do it while at the same time talking to a friend, listening to the radio, singing out load, or smoking a cigarette.

Had the risk of crashing disappeared?

No, but you were better able to deal with the risk, because you developed a degree of mastery with the new behavior.

It's the same thing with investing. People find it scary at first and think it is very risky. But instead of using the same process they used when learning to drive, they decide to manage their risk by doing nothing at all. If they just went through the process of learning, doing, adapting, and repeating, the risk of investing would diminish, just as it did when learning to drive a car.

Yes, there is still risk, and there always will be, but with practice you can minimize risks to the point where you hardly notice them, and you can confidently take action without becoming immobilized by fear.

FAIL FORWARD FAST

Failing is so misunderstood! Most of us do everything we can to avoid it, and of course, we end up failing anyway in some aspect of our lives. We have been taught that failing at something means *we* are failures or *we* will never be successful. Whereas if we realized that it is only through failing that we ever learn anything new, we would have confidence to try new things. This switch in perspective can empower you to take control over your own financial future rather than leaving it someone else's hands.

If you take a look around at some of the things we take for granted today, such as electric light bulbs, airplane travel, television, phones, the Internet, and, to be fair, just about everything else in our lives, you would soon see that these things would never exist if it weren't for the fact that someone was willing to fail. It's been reported that Thomas Edison failed 10,000 times in his quest to invent the incandescent light bulb. Did he fail though? Or did he just learn 9,999 ways that didn't work? Was he only successful on his last attempt, or was it a 9,999-step process to success that never could have been accomplished if not for what he had learned through his previous "failures"?

It's the same with the Wright brothers. Did they only succeed the last time when they got the plane airborne? Or was it the knowledge they gained from every failure —or learning experience—that ultimately led to their final success?

You can look at any successful businessperson or investor, and you would find that early on they had what most of us call failures or setbacks. However, successful people do not see these events as failures. They see them as opportunities to learn and move forward confidently with the knowledge of what went wrong and what they can do differently in the future. The critical error that most of us make is never starting out on the journey of financial success, because we are too afraid of making mistakes and being seen as failures. In doing this, we deprive ourselves of opportunities to learn from our mistakes. Ironically, this only sets the stage for us to fail later in life. The problem is that by then, there is very often no time left to make amends and learn.

Failing is not the enemy; it is made out to be, but it is actually one of the best ways to learn. This understanding can help us to make better decisions for our financial futures than the ones the majority of us are making right now.

Imagine this scenario: You are about a year old, and you've just gained the confidence to stand up by holding onto your mother's hand or a piece of furniture. Emboldened by this success, you now decide that it is time to go for it, and take that first unaided step. Off you go, and you fall. Maybe you even hurt yourself. Basically, you fail! And now you decide that because you have failed you will never, ever try walking again! Ridiculous as this may seem, it's what most of us do with our money every single day.

RISK VERSUS REWARD

The rewards you get in life are in direct proportion to the risks you take.

However, most people think risk-taking means you have to gamble to succeed. Taking risk is not the same as gambling. Donald Trump, Richard Branson, and

Warren Buffet *do not* gamble with their money. They take *calculated risks* with their money, and they reap the rewards.

Learning to take control of your own financial destiny, and experiencing the joy of succeeding at something new will naturally build your self-confidence. The reward of seld-confidence will further enable you to move forward intelligently, rather than relying on others to invest for you.

In addition to asking yourself what could go wrong, make sure you ask these quality questions as well:

What could go right?

What if it works?

What could I learn?

What difference will I make in my life and in the life of my family by learning how to invest for financial security?

KEEPING PACE WITH INFLATION

The old advice of work hard, pay off your mortgage, and save into a retirement plan for retirement is not as safe as you think. With these "safe" strategies your money is actually under serious threat, because the cost of living, or inflation, is eroding the real value of your money over time.

The cost of living is rising far faster than wage inflation, which explains why people find it harder to save money for retirement.

The government hides the real cost of living, quoting instead the inflation rate, or the Consumer Price Index. This monthly figure does not include things such as food, heating, fuel costs, or housing costs. Instead it is based on a limited basket of goods. We all know and can see quite clearly that the real cost of living is rising far faster than the inflation rate the government reports to us.

So, if we are putting our money into "cautious" savings plans, and these "cautious" savings plans do not keep pace with the cost of living year by year, the value of our money is actually being eroded year after year and has to work far harder and gain higher returns just to keep up with the cost of living.

This is why it is even more important in today's economy that we learn how to invest our money and how to take a more active role in creating our own financial futures. We have to increase the returns we reap just to survive. To stay ahead of the cost of living increases that are happening all around us, we have to make better and more informed decisions with our money.

MINIMIZE RISK AND TAKE THE FEAR AWAY

Learning how to invest with minimum risk will take away the fear of planning, and allow you to take advantage of more better ways to save for your retirement.

There is no such thing as an investment without risk; but through knowledge and education—and by doing, learning, and adapting new strategies as you go—you can effectively understand and minimize these risks.

As I've said elsewhere in this book, giving away control of your financial future is by far the riskiest form of financial planning of all, and yet, it is the route taken by the majority of people. Learning how to take control yourself, and investing in your own education requires more effort in the beginning, but once learned, you greatly increase your chances of working less, enjoying a higher quality of life, and retiring sooner.

MONEY PUZZLE MASTERY
EXERCISES—RISK

After reading this chapter and seriously thinking about its content, what are the three most important things that you need to remember about *risk*?

1. _____
2. _____
3. _____

How has learning this affected the way you think about your financial future?

_____
_____
_____
_____

As a result of what you have learned in this chapter, what actions do you intend to take in order to create a more successful and abundant future?

1. _____
2. _____
3. _____
4. _____
5. _____

Describe a time when you learned something new.

_____
_____
_____
_____

What steps did you take? What happened along the way?

_____

_____

_____

_____

How did you feel in the beginning?

_____

_____

_____

_____

How did you feel once you had become proficient?

_____

_____

_____

_____

BUILD YOUR OWN ASSETS

BUILD YOUR OWN ASSETS TO CREATE THE INCOME YOU DESIRE

> *"Rule One. You must know the difference between an asset and a liability, and buy assets. The poor and middle class acquire liabilities, but they think they are assets. An asset is something that puts money in my pocket. A liability is something that takes money out of my pocket"*
>
> —*Robert Kiyosaki*

BECAUSE you are creating your own resources and not relying on anyone else to provide your future financial security, building your own assets is the only sure-fire way to become financially independent.

The other choice is to relinquish control of your financial future to a company or the government, but as we've seen, neither of these entities have anywhere near the same concern for you as they do for themselves.

By taking control of your own retirement planning you will be working your own plan and nobody else's. This will put you in a far better position to create what you're really after: passive income that comes to you day after day, month after month, year after year without you ever needing to work for it again.

You will have achieved real financial independence when you've built up enough assets that can be invested at a reasonable rate of return and provide you with a consistent monthly income.

As I mentioned at the end of the Retirement chapter, the three main asset classes for creating wealth are business, shares, and property.

Everybody has his or her own opinion about which asset class is best, and stories abound about people who have made millions in each of the asset classes.

Before we discuss each of these methods, you should know up front that I firmly believe that property is the best asset class of all for the majority of people who want to build real long term wealth and financial security.

WHAT ABOUT SHARES?

There is money to be made in shares, and there are a lot of excellent educational systems that can guide you through the steps to creating wealth in this area.

Before you invest your money in shares, however, you should be aware that, in my experience, to make good returns in the stock market you will have to work really hard, and you will need to do an enormous amount of research on a continual basis.

You will need to update your research, probably daily, and amend and update your system on a daily basis, too. Investing in shares is a very active business, and although you can make some fantastic returns on the shares you invest in, you will have to be prepared to see things go against you sometimes.

In his book, *Multiple Streams of Income*, Robert Allen says:

"You may be surprised to learn that 75 percent of all the smartest money managers in the world, working twenty-hour days, with huge research staffs, powered by the most advanced computers, have not been able to consistently beat the market. Of the remaining 25 percent, most were just able to keep pace with the market (but when you factor in commissions and fees you're still a net loser). In the history of the markets, only a tiny number of long-term superstars, out of millions who have tried, have been able to tame this tiger. That's why they are so famous and rich."

Shares can be a very powerful way to build assets if you know what you are doing. Most people's idea of investing in the stock market is to invest in mutual funds and pooled investments through their bank or insurance company. This isn't really investing in the stock market, as you are giving total control away to somebody else to invest your money for you. If you don't know what you are doing with the stock market, you stand to lose a lot of money very quickly.

There are an enormous amount of different strategies and methods for investing in the stock market using both fundamental analysis and technical analysis techniques. There are over 10,000 individual stocks trading on the American

Stock Exchange alone. The question is how to screen and filter all of these stocks effectively in order to even find the investments that have the potential to make you money. It is not just about buying low and selling high either, as there are many methods of investing that allow you to make money from stocks that are going up, down, or sideways in the market.

The stock market is also a very volatile place to invest. This means that picking the right stocks can make you a lot of money in a short amount of time, but it also can mean that any money you do make can quite quickly get wiped out. So, even if you are one of the few who really make a huge amount of money in the stock market, you have to still be aware that your investment can fall in value very fast indeed, and if you are relying on this money to create the income you need in retirement, you may be left with a far lower standard of living or having to wait until the value of your stocks rise again, if they ever do!

Because of this, I firmly believe that for the majority of us it is very difficult to make a great deal of money in the stock market.

However, if the stock market is appealing to you as an asset, I recommend that you take a small portion of the funds you have available to invest and learn the strategies to invest in the stock market yourself. Starting small will help you learn the pitfalls as well as the advantages to investing in the stock market without taking big risks with a huge amount of money. As you continue to build confidence and knowledge, you can start to build momentum by using more available resources to compound the growth of your money.

If you haven't got a great deal of starting capital, the stock market does allow you to take small amounts of money and, if invested wisely, turn them into larger amounts of money. It can be a very good asset class to start accumulating the funds required to invest in the other asset classes, as well.

So, don't disregard the stock market completely, as you may be missing out on the growth of not just your money but in the skills you will gain by learning how to invest wisely. Do not, however, jump in too soon to investing in this asset class, as you may get burned very quickly by investing without sufficient knowledge and education.

WHAT ABOUT BUSINESS?

A highly successful business can build untold wealth and riches, and often they start with something most people have every day—a great idea.

Think about the great businesses that exist today—Microsoft and Google, for instance—that started from humble beginnings as an idea in someone's mind. In a relatively short period of time, these ideas created billions for their respective owners —Bill Gates and Paul Allen for Microsoft, and Sergey Brin and Larry Page for Google.

Think also of some of the more traditional businesses such as Wal-Mart, Marks and Spencer, and Sony that also started out with great ideas and humble beginnings, and grew into the huge corporations we know today.

Creating your own business can also be more rewarding as an asset than shares or property, because it can simultaneously provide personal growth as well as monetary rewards. To see your idea come to fruition and provide service in the world is enormously satisfying. And to be sure, running your own business and having complete control over the income you earn and the hours you keep is far more inspiring than turning up to work for someone else every day for the rest of your working life.

I really believe that inside all of us there is an idea for a great business that has the potential to free us from the shackles of working for someone else. It's just that some people act on their ideas, while others shy away from taking the necessary steps to get their ideas to market. Have you ever seen a product or service come to market and say to yourself, "I thought of that once."?

Well, apparently, somebody else thought of it too, but instead of pushing it to the back of her mind, that person took the first steps that eventually created a lucrative business.

Before starting out on your new business venture, however, you need to be aware of the odds, because in all honesty, the statistics are staggering. In his book, *Keys to the Vault: Lessons from the Pros on Raising Money and Igniting Your Business,* Keith Cunningham tells us that "50 percent of all new business start-ups will be gone within a couple of years, and 80 percent will not celebrate a fifth anniversary."

Transforming a great idea into a profitable business can be more work than you ever imagined, and you need to realize that at least in the beginning, you will probably work far more hours a day than you ever would if you were working for someone else. If you're successful, you will be rewarded—both personally and monetarily—in far greater amounts than you could ever expect to receive from working in a job. If you're unsuccessful, you will unfortunately join the 80percent of businesses that fail.

Regardless of what business you are in, nothing happens without marketing.

So, you could say that whatever business you are in, you are really in the marketing business. Whether you are providing information, selling a service or a product, or running a professional, manufacturing, or retail business, you will not keep your doors open—virtual or otherwise—without marketing in some shape or form. All businesses need marketing to be successful, and yet this is the activity that is least understood and pursued by most businesses—even very successful ones.

Gerry Robert, a marketing genius and the author of several books including the fantastic *The Millionaire Mindset—How Ordinary People Create Extraordinary Income*, explains in his latest book *Multiply Your Business* how radically the consumer mindset has changed, and how traditional advertising and marketing are largely obsolete in today's world. He writes:

> "There are new marketing realities. Those who know about these critical shifts in the marketplace can capitalize upon them; those who don't are destined to continue to suffer poor business performance or even perish in the marketplace."

In today's world of excessive advertising, where information comes at us from all angles twenty-four hours a day, it's no wonder that the consumer mindset has changed. We have far more choices now than ever before, and in our Internet age we are bombarded with a constant stream of advertising and purchasing choices.

So, when thinking about starting or investing in a business, it is imperative that you employ a marketing plan that can cut through the mass of marketing "noise" that is out there and attract your client to you. You have to get through to the people who are already predisposed to buying your product or service instead of blanket-marketing to the masses who are not likely to be interested in what you have to offer.

Your potential customers are more informed, more sceptical, and more demanding than ever before. They are also less loyal, less trusting, and less gullible than ever before. So, the old marketing strategies of manipulating customers, cold-calling masses of people, and relying on a "numbers game" to covert leads into sales is just not going to cut it in today's marketplace. Instead of chasing customers, you need to get them coming to you with their hands raised high, saying that they are interested in what you have to offer. You must establish credibility, get your message heard, increase client trust, and make sure your business stands out from the crowd. Your marketing message needs to quickly and clearly demonstrate the benefits of your product or service, and it has to do this amidst the cacophony of the other marketing messages that are baying for people's attention today.

You have to be innovative in developing your product or service so that it provides exactly what your ideal client is seeking. You have to figure out how to reach your ideal client, educate them about what you do, show them how you can help them, and how you are different from your competition. People today are wary of shelling out their hard-earned cash, so the more quickly you can help them trust you, and the more they grow to depend upon your product or service to provide them with the benefits they want, the more your business will flourish and your profits will grow.

In the end, people really do not care about you, your company, your product, or your service. They care about themselves, their problems, their families, and most of all, their money. And yet, most marketing messages are still full of information about how knowledgeable you are and how wonderful your company is. Marketing has to address your customers' desires, and it has to feature the things that are of greatest interest to them. And in order to speak to their needs, of course, you first have to understand them.

It's staggering to consider the mass of money that is spent each year on advertisements that are in our face one minute, and in the trash bin the next. Your marketing approach needs to have a longer shelf life if you want to really grow a successful business. You need to be seen regularly and frequently by your ideal client. And, most of all, you need to reach your clients in the most cost-effective way possible.

If you can do all of this, you will have the best chance of running a successful and profitable business. If you can't, you may end up in the 80 percent crowd. After reading all this, if you find that you're still eager to move forward with a business endeavour, I would offer you the following advice:

Before you even start out in business—even if you have a great idea for a product or service that could benefit millions of people—you have to get your marketing strategy right. Remember, it doesn't matter what business you are in, you are really in the marketing business, so marketing has to be your top priority. Unless you are seen as a credible person who offers a unique product or service that can solve people's problems, then you are likely to struggle in today's world.

Dan Sullivan, in his program *The D.O.S. Conversation,* says that " ... Products and services will be increasingly sold on the basis of price, and this type of business only really suits the big players who profit at reduced prices through economies of scale and huge marketing budgets. For entrepreneurs who can't compete with the Amazon.coms and Charles Schwabs of their industries, the challenge is to differentiate themselves from the competition and make a profit. The entrepreneurs who are truly thriving are doing so by creating unique value for their clients and customers."

Because of technology, the Internet especially, and the increasing numbers of merchants in the marketplace, most products and services are gradually becoming commoditized, meaning they are being sold on the basis of price alone. You escape commoditization through creating exceptional value for your clients by doing something that clearly differentiates you from your competition, and at the same time justifies what you charge for your product or service. Your success in business will ultimately depend on developing long-term relationships with clients and customers. Creating value, innovation, and differentiation in what you offer has to be of paramount importance.

PROPERTY—YOUR ROUTE TO FINANCIAL INDEPENDENCE

PROPERTY AND THE POWER OF LEVERAGE

The leverage you can gain with property makes it one of the best asset classes to invest in: first, because it enables you to buy far more for your money, and second, because it allows you to control and own an asset worth far more than your starting capital. The returns you receive are not only based on your capital investment, but on the whole asset that you own.

Put simply, property gives you more return for your money, or more "bang" for your buck.

Let's say that you have $50,000. If you invested it in savings, you would own$50,000 worth of savings. If you invested it in shares, you would own $50,000 worth of shares.

However, if you invested it in property, you could leverage your $50,000, and use it as a deposit on property worth $333,000. Rather than owning only $50,000 of property, you own the whole $333,000 value of the property!

Now, let's imagine that all of the asset classes—savings, shares, and property—went up by 5percent in value. With your savings, your value would increase by $2,500. With your shares, your value would increase by $2,500. However, with property, your value would increase by **$16,650,** because you leveraged your initial capital using other people's money (mortgage finance from the bank).

That's a massive 566% more return on the initial investment of money!

Granted, you have to borrow money to leverage your own capital, and you will pay a monthly amount of interest for borrowing this money. But that's the other great leverage bonus with property: by renting the property out, somebody else actually pays the mortgage for you!

You can not only leverage your capital by borrowing money to buy a bigger asset, but you can leverage someone else's money to pay the finance charges on what you have borrowed.

THE SUPPLY AND DEMAND OF PROPERTY

We are an ever-expanding population. The U.S. Census Bureau published statistics showing that the population in the United States is currently 310 million, and is set to rise to 373 million by 2030, and to 439 million by 2050. This is a rise of 63 million people in just twenty years! And in 2007, the U.K. Government Actuary's Department predicted that the population in the U.K. would rise to 71 million by 2031. That's an increase of more than 10 million in just over twenty years!

These statistics show clearly that there is going to be a continuing and rising demand for property, because our rising populations will always need somewhere to live and work.

Because of improved standards of living and medical advancements, people are living in their homes for far longer than ever before, which puts a big restriction on the supply of resale homes. Furthermore, when somebody does die, the property doesn't always comes onto the market, because more people now realize that property is a great investment, and opt to keep it rather than sell it.

So, if we are not making any more land, not releasing enough of our existing land, not building enough new homes, and our older homes are not coming onto the market as frequently, this can only mean that the demand for housing is going to continue to outstrip supply. Therefore, as an asset, the value is going to go up.

INVESTMENT PROPERTY WILL UNDERPIN THE PROPERTY MARKET

A lot of people say that the housing market cannot keep going up because it would prevent first-time buyers from ever being able to afford to buy. But as prices go up and first-time buyers are not able to buy, more and more people will need to rent.

These "would-have-been first-time buyers" still need to live somewhere, meaning they will rent homes longer. The investment property market has also grown substantially over the last ten years, as more and more people realize the power of property—both as an investment, and as a replacement for retirement provision.

The availability of investment mortgages has also grown substantially, and even in our current financial environment this has helped many people who would not have been able to invest in property twenty years ago, invest in property.

There has also been a shift toward more people renting, because it is more socially acceptable to rent these days than it was twenty years ago. In addition, people now move around more frequently for jobs, so renting provides an easier alternative to selling houses every time their jobs move.

Overall, I believe the property market will not only be underpinned by the first-time buyers, but will be helped substantially by the ever-growing number of property investors that see property as a fantastic and very real way of making money in the long term.

UNDERSTAND HOW PROPERTY FITS INTO YOUR CHOICES

There are many possibilities for leveraging property to widen the choices that are available to you for retirement planning. All of these options can provide you with much more income in retirement than any pension plan or savings plan could ever hope to provide. Let's look at some of the benefits:

- Property as an asset class provides the potential for a rising passive income from rentals each year that over time will provide a regular income from the investment.
- Property offers great capital growth potential over the long term.
- Property is an asset that allows you to leverage your own starting capital

and therefore enjoy the growth of an asset far greater than the original capital invested.

- Property offers the potential to continue to leverage the asset by using equity in one property to fund the purchase of additional properties, therefore increasing the overall asset value that you own.

- Property provides far more flexibility for your retirement in that your money is not locked away as it is in a pension. You get to choose when to buy, when to sell, and when to retire, and furthermore, you can leave the full value of your properties and the income from them to your dependents after you die.

A WEALTHY RETIREMENT THROUGH PROPERTY ASSETS

Building property assets is the most powerful way of creating a wealthy retirement, because you can continue to leverage your capital by using the equity accumulated in one property to purchase additional properties.

For example, let's say you currently own a house valued at $150,000 with a mortgage of $80,000, thus leaving you with equity in this property of $70,000.

Now, let's say this property increases in value at just 5 percent per year over the next twenty years. This property would be valued at nearly $400,000 in twenty years.

Of course, that's great news. But what if you were to move $40,000 equity out of this house today, and buy additional property with this money? You would be able to buy up to $260,000 worth of additional property from the same equity that you currently own.

Again, assuming that these properties grow at just 5percent per year over the next twenty years, your total assets would now be worth just over 1 millioin, and you would have just made nearly $700,000 in additional equity— money that is yours to do with what you like—all from the same initial equity you owned in the beginning.

And, as the value of your properties increases over the years, you can continue to use the equity you build to add assets that will contribute even more to your retirement fund.

Work out how much per month you would have to save into a retirement fund in order to create a fund worth $700,000 in twenty years. I'll bet that you will not be able to afford it, or even if you could, you wouldn't be able to put that much into it anyway because of the limits imposed on how much you are allowed to save into your retirement fund!

THE PAST AND FUTURE FOR HOUSE PRICES

By understanding housing trends, it's easy to see why property is such a powerful investment. You can examine the actual figures for what they are without getting caught up in either negative or overly positive press.

By looking at the hard facts and figures on the growth of home prices, you can see the *truth*, and you can make your own decisions rather than be swayed by the opinions of someone else whose job it is to sell newspapers.

The facts are that the average United States new home price in 1963 was $19,300. In 2007 this average home price in the United States had risen to $313,600. These figures show an average yearly increase of 6.63 percent, and an average ten-year home price increase of 92percent.

This means that over this forty-four-year period, house prices in the United States have nearly doubled in value every ten years.

(Source: www.census.gov/const/uspriceann.pdf)

Also, the average U.K. home price in 1946 was £1459. In 2007 this average home price in the U.K. had risen to £221,580. These figures show an average yearly increase in house price of 8.86percent, and an average ten-year house price increase of 140.46 percent.

This means that over the last sixty-one years house prices in the U.K .have not just doubled in value in each ten-year period, but have doubled, and then grown by nearly half again.

(Source – Communities.gov.uk – Table 502)

These figures show excellent returns as they are. But when you take into account leverage, and the fact that you are able to own the full value of property as an asset with relatively little—and in some cases none—of your own money, you will see that the potential returns on your money are far greater than the average house price figures suggest.

If you look at these figures, review the past trends, and consider them in relation to future trends such as population growth, housing supply and demand, our ageing population, and immigration, you will see that the odds of house prices continuing to grow consistently are very good indeed.

THE TWO POTENT FORCES: COMPOUNDING AND LEVERAGE

As we discussed earlier, compound interest is a very powerful force. Einstein called it the Eighth Wonder of the World.

We also saw earlier that when it comes to investing money, leverage is another powerful force, as it escalates the return on your money, allowing you to buy assets worth more than the original capital that you start out with.

When combined together, these two potent forces can be used to your advantage to create massive wealth. They build upon each other, creating greater asset values, which in turn give you more opportunity to leverage and buy more assets. This cycle of wealth building is virtually unstoppable, and can grow your net worth exponentially.

Consider this with respect to the average property figures shown above.

Let's say that someone in the U.S. bought a house for cash in 1963 for $19,300 with absolutely no leverage at all. With compound growth being the force that it is, the investment of $19,300 would now have grown to $313,600.

Now, let's say that they had leveraged their money just once in 1963, and used this $19,300 as 15percent deposits on property. Instead of being able to buy just the one property for $19,300, this person would now have been in a position to purchase property to the value of $128,538.

Without any more leveraging of the property values at all, the property values would now be worth $1.9 *million*.

This is more than six times higher growth from the same starting capital of $19,300, and this person would have built up $1.6 million in extra wealth today!

Let's say that someone in the U.K. bought a house for cash in 1946 for £1459, and they bought it with absolutely no leverage at all. With compound growth being the force that it is, the investment of £1459 would now have grown to £221,580.

Now, let's say that they had leveraged their money just once in 1946, and used this £1459 as 15percent deposit on property. Instead of being able to buy just the one property for £1459, this person would now have been in a position to purchase property to the value of £9716.

Without any more leveraging of the property values at all, the property values would now be worth £1,465,852.

This is nearly seven times higher growth from the same starting capital of £1459, and this person would have built up £1,244,273 in extra wealth today!

As you can see, the two potent forces of compounding and leverage acting together will make a significant difference to your wealth.

BUILDING EQUITY INSTEAD OF A PENSION

There are four main reasons why investing in property and building equity can be a far better route to a secure retirement than saving your money into a pension fund:

- Property gives you infinitely more opportunity to leverage your money, not just on the initial purchase, but the ongoing leverage of being able to use your money to create more assets.
- Property, unlike a pension fund, gives you more control over how your money grows and gives you far more choices as to how you can personally affect the value of your assets.
- You have far more choice as to what you can do with the equity in property when you retire than you have within a pension fund.
- Pension funds mainly provide capital growth, whereas property offers the increase in rental values over time, which can build up a passive income without needing to access the equity growth. Let's look at an example of this:

Let's say you bought a property today valued at $150,000 with an 85 percent mortgage of 127.5k. At 6 percent interest, your monthly payment would be $637 if you are paying interest only. Let's say you were able to rent out this property for $650 per month. If rental values went up by just 5 percent per year, then the monthly rent you would receive twenty years from now would be $1724 per month. Less your mortgage payment of $637 this means you would now be generating $1087 per month in passive income. This is on top of the fact that the property would then be worth nearly 400k, assuming a 5 percent average annual growth rate.

ADVANTAGES AND DISADVANTAGES OF PROPERTY

The disadvantages of investing in property as an asset are very small compared to all of the advantages. However, I will touch on them briefly so you can make an informed decision:

Property can be an illiquid asset. This means that should you wish to sell the asset in order to release the cash in the property, it usually takes some time before you actually get money into your hands.

You also have to consider the time and money required to maintain the property, and the fact that property ownership will require you to deal with tenants, tradesmen, property management agents, etcetera. You may also encounter some problem tenants along the way that need special attention.

However, weighing the disadvantages compared to the benefits of leverage; compound growth on an asset far bigger than your initial starting capital; tenants paying your mortgage for you; and the myriad of choices as to what you can do with your equity fund once you've built it, it's quite easy to see that property as an investment vehicle in an excellent choice for creating long term wealth.

Considering the disadvantages of retirement funds and the lack of control over solutions to improve them, it's easy to see that the disadvantages of property as an investment are far easier to deal with and overcome, especially if you buy the right property in the first place, and you have planned for the risks in advance.

The only advantage to a pension fund is that it's easy in that you don't have to think about it. You put your money in each month and do nothing else until it's time to retire. However, as we've seen, this ease far too often degenerates into complacency, and many people only realize the disadvantages of investing their money in this way after it's too late to resolve them.

THE TIME TO SELL PROPERTY

Knowing the right time to sell your property is an important skill to hone. People often sell property when they don't need to, and end up giving away an asset to someone else who will benefit from its future growth. On the contrary, people sometimes hold onto property when they could benefit much more by selling it and creating more growth potential for the future.

It's important to have exit strategies for all your investments. This will ensure that if you no longer want to keep managing your properties, you can sell your portfolio and put your money into income-creating, cash-based investments that you can live on for the rest of your life.

As you consider whether or not to sell a property, you must take into account the current tax regime, because you will be liable to pay any tax on your gains. Therefore, it's important to factor your tax liability into any plans you have when selling property.

In truth, the only three occasions where I believe it could be advantageous to sell your property are:

- If the neighbourhood where your property is located is declining, as this may have a significant impact on property values in the future
- If you know that you can earn far greater returns by putting the equity you own into a better performing property asset (and if you don't have other resources available to make this investment without selling the property)
- If you want to cash in the equity and live on the interest from the gains that you have made

Overall, selling a property is the worst thing you can ever do for your wealth. If you sell an investment property that has gone up in value, you will pay tax on the gains you make. However, if you keep the property and leverage the equity instead of selling, you will pay no tax on this money because you do not have to pay tax on money you borrow.

Also, if you sell a property today, you are basically giving away its potential future growth to the person who buys it from you. As we saw earlier, the average ten-year house price has risen by 92 percent in the U.S. and 140 percent in the U.K., and so if you sell a property today for $150,000, and we assume that property continues to grow at the same rate, you are giving away a potential $138,000 in the U.S. and $210,000 in the U.K. over the next ten years to the person who buys it from you.

Most people who are moving do not realize that they could keep their existing home as a rental property and still be able to release the equity they need to buy their new home as well as grow their future financial security.

UNDERSTANDING WHEN TO KEEP PROPERTY

If you look at the past performance of property as an asset, and take into account the leverage that property affords you, in most cases it's easy to see how foolish it is to sell an asset that is going to continue to rise in value and further enhance your wealth year after year after year.

As I said, the only time you ever pay tax on your gains is when you sell. In addition to giving away any future growth to someone else, why would you give away any of your gains to the tax man?

The other thing you lose when you sell a property is the income that you earn from the rent. As we saw earlier, passive income over time increases as rents increase, and mortgage payments remain stable. So, even though you may find cashing in your equity and putting it in an income-producing cash investment to be an attractive option, don't forget that you could be losing a great deal of future income to get to this position.

Let's take an example. Let's say you bought a house today worth $150,000 and rented it out for $750 per month. Let's say that your mortgage payment was also $750 per month today. In this case you would not be earning any passive income from the property today because the income is only covering the expense.

Now, let's assume that you are thirty years old, and that you aim to retire at age 65. Assuming a 5 percent annual average growth rate, the property you just purchased will be worth more than $800,000 in thirty-five years. Your mortgage, assuming no additional borrowing, and that it has been an interest-only mortgage, is still only 150k.

This means that you now have equity of more than $650,000. You may think that selling would be a good idea, because you could put this equity in the bank and earn 5percent interest, giving you a monthly income of $2,822. But what have you lost in doing this? Assuming the rental income grew at 5percent per annum, the rental income from this property would be $4,137 per month in thirty-five years. Your mortgage payment is likely to still be around $750 per month, because although mortgage rates fluctuate, they don't rise each year with inflation or the cost of living. So, you would be getting $3,387 in passive income from the property.

And you still have retained the $650,000-plus equity in a property worth over $800,000 that would continue to grow in value for you while providing you an income. In five years time, if the property continued to grow at just 5 percent per year, this property that you would have otherwise sold would now be worth over a million dollars. So, by selling, you would also be losing nearly $250,000 in just five years on top of the continued rental income.

Even though there are certain circumstances that warrant the sale of property, you must always weigh the potential losses with the benefits of keeping your property for the long term. It's usually the best choice you can make to continue building and keeping your wealth.

Because we are now living longer, one of the biggest issues facing people is how to get additional income that will see them through the rest of their lives. Many people are trying to release the equity from their homes to use for income. You might say they are in a lucky position—except, if they had the foresight to have taken that equity earlier and purchased at least one other property—they would now have far greater resources available to them without having to take equity from their homes.

YOU CAN PERSONALLY AFFECT THE VALUE OF PROPERTY

When it comes to all of the asset classes you can invest in to build wealth, property is the best asset for offering the opportunity to add value to your investment personally. You can personally increase the value of your asset without even waiting for average annual increases in property values.

If you invest your money into a pension fund, there is absolutely nothing you can do to increase the value of your investment; you are simply bound by the investment growth of the fund over time. If you invest in shares, you can actively buy and sell effectively as the share price moves, in order to make money, but you cannot physically affect the value of the share itself.

If you were to invest in a business, there are things that you can personally do to increase the value of your business over time—invest more money in marketing to bring in new customers, increase the number of employees, add new product lines, reduce costs, etcetera. But even with all of these changes, a business is a much harder asset to assess the value of, and this makes it difficult to predict the gains you can expect to earn as a result of making these changes.

Property, however, is an asset that is more easily valued to begin with, so it is much easier to know what you stand to gain by making any personal changes in order to affect the value of the property.

So, what can you personally do to affect the value of a property even before average increases in prices kick in and increase its value over the long term?

Well, just think for a moment, and I'll bet you could come up with dozens of ways that you could improve the value of property. You can extend it, add a bedroom, convert the loft, change the windows, paint and decorate throughout, add a new kitchen, a new bathroom, convert a garage, add a conservatory, landscape the garden, create parking space, or change the guttering. You could even completely renovate an old and dilapidated building.

These, and hundreds of others, are things that you can personally do to increase the value of a property, all of which will create an equity fund in the property that will then continue to grow over the long term to bring you massive wealth.

And, if home improvement isn't your thing, the good news is that you don't have to do anything to the property itself to create equity. By finding the right opportunity, you could buy the property under market value and create equity instantly.

WHY IS LEARNING ABOUT PROPERTY EASIER THAN ANY OTHER ASSET CLASS?

In my experience, the majority of people find it far easier to understand the investment benefits of buying property than to understand shares or business as investment assets.

This is because most people have had some experience with the buying and selling of property, and most have had experience maintaining a property.

Because most people already have some experience and understanding of property, it doesn't take too long to build the confidence to purchase their first investment property.

And, once you buy your first investment property, your knowledge base increases, and with it, your confidence. Eventually, this skill develops into an ever-increasing cycle for success.

THE CASH FLOW OF PROPERTY

Understanding cash flow is critical to determining whether a property is a good investment or not.

Most people focus on the capital growth of property, and while this is an important part of property investment, it is actually not the most important component to understand.

The reason you need to look at the cash flow of property is that you could end up buying a property that goes up significantly in value, but if the cash flowing into and out of the property puts your finances at risk; it could become a liability rather than an asset.

It is also a good idea to compare the cash flow with property against the cash flow of other investments such as retirement plans, shares, and business.

If you look at property with regard to the purchase of your own home, the cash flow normally goes like this:

You buy the home using a deposit of money that flows from you through your solicitor to the person from whom you are buying the property. You then take a mortgage out to finance the rest of the purchase. The money from the bank flows to your solicitor and on to the seller of the property. You now own the property and you also have a mortgage on which your bank or building society will charge you interest each month. You will make your mortgage payment every month; otherwise you will lose the property. Where do you get the cash flow to make the payment? From the cash that flows in to your bank account from your job, a business, investments, etcetera.

It doesn't matter how much the property rises in value, because all that's ever going to happen with your own home is that cash is going to flow out of your pocket and into someone else's—i.e., the bank or building society—until you have repaid the mortgage. On top of this, the cash flows out of your pocket for property tax, utilities, and maintenance, as well.

So, when most people think of their home as their biggest investment, they are in fact totally and completely misguided. It is more accurate to say that a home is their biggest liability because it strips them of their cash every month.

Now, compare this to an investment property. You buy the property and again put a deposit down, so this cash still flows from you to the seller. You again take out a mortgage to finance the rest, so the bank or building society funds still flow in the same direction—to the seller. But now, you rent out the property instead of living in it. You still have to pay the mortgage, so the money flows out of your bank to make the payment. But now you have money flowing *into* your bank from the person renting the property, which covers the cost your mortgage payment— in part or in whole. So now, it's your renter's hard-earned cash rather than your own that is paying the mortgage lender.

On top of this, the tenant also pays the property taxes and utilities on the property, so it's someone else's cash, not yours, that is maintaining the property for you while it increases in value over time to create an equity fund for your future financial well-being.

THE NINE STEPS TO SUCCESSFUL PROPERTY INVESTING

Whether you decide to invest in the stock market, in a business, or in property to build a more prosperous future, there are certain steps that you should follow in order to maximize success and minimize risks. The following steps are what I believe should be taken when investing in property, and these steps can be applied to investing in shares and business too. You need to:

1. Decide to become an investor
2. Decide to get educated
3. Calculate your purchasing fund
4. Decide on strategy
5. Find an ideal area in which to buy
6. Identify/Analyze properties
7. Negotiate the deal
8. Fund the deal
9 Manage the property

1. **Decide to become an investor**
    You have to make the commitment to take responsibility for your own financial future, and therefore, to become an investor. I hope I've given you more than enough reasons to take this important first step. If you don't become an investor and do what you can to create your own wealth, your future financial well-being is left in other people's hands. And as we have already seen, this could be the most risky thing you ever do.

2. **Decide to get educated**
    You have made the first step in your education by picking up this book and reading it to this point. I hope you have learned enough so far to start taking control of your own financial destiny. However, I really believe this is just the first step in the process. No one is ever educated enough to stop learning in life. The world continually moves on, so those who believe they no longer need to learn might find themselves in a world where they are left behind.

Education comes in many forms, for example, books, seminars, and personal coaching, just to name a few. Learning also comes from experience, which is the most powerful form of education. We can read books all day or go to as many seminars as we are able, but this type of learning is all conceptual. It isn't until we "get our hands dirty" and amass real-life experience that we learn the things we need to learn in life.

3. **Calculate your purchasing fund**

Before you can even begin to look at investment properties, you have to be clear about your current financial situation. You must know exactly how much money you have in order to calculate how much money you can put toward creating the life of your dreams.

If you didn't do the exercises that were presented earlier in the book, do them now. Work out exactly where you are today and where you want to be when the time comes for you to retire. Mapping this out will make it much easier to work out the plan to get there. Once you have a clear picture of your current finances, it is possible to calculate the purchasing fund that you have at your disposal in order to bridge the gap from where you are to where you want to be.

To determine your purchasing fund and how much property you can safely buy, I recommend you sit down with an experienced mortgage broker who understands property as an investment and can help you find the right financing strategies for your situation.

4. **Decide on your Strategy**

Once you know what funds you have available to invest, you can turn your attention to some of the different strategies available to create wealth in property. Start to consider the following:

- ✓ Do I buy an apartment to let out to professionals?
- ✓ Do I buy a family home to let out to families?
- ✓ Do I buy a property with 2, 3, 4, or 5 bedrooms?
- ✓ Do I buy a property that needs complete refurbishment?
- ✓ Do I buy a property to extend or improve?
- ✓ Do I buy a plot of land to build a house on from scratch?
- ✓ Do I buy a bigger plot of land and develop more properties?

✓ Do I buy a piece of land with no planning permission and obtain planning permission that will increase the property's value?

✓ Do I buy repossession properties?

✓ Do I buy newly built properties from developers?

✓ Do I buy commercial property? If so, what type of commercial property would suit me?

✓ Do I invest all on my own?

✓ Do I team up and joint venture with others?

✓ Do I look for investment opportunities that I can invest in without doing the actual investing myself?

✓ What is my exit strategy?

When deciding upon your strategy, it's important to consider both your long-term and short-term goals. It is also important to consider how much time you have to devote to investing in your future, and to weigh the pros and cons of each strategy before deciding to implement any particular one. Depending on your starting position, you may decide on one strategy with the idea that you'll move onto others as your wealth builds; or you may decide that you can encompass a few strategies right from the start. This is why it is so important that you first determine your starting position.

Your overall strategy should include an exit strategy for the investment property. When I say exit strategy, I don't really mean when you plan to sell the property because, as we discussed earlier, there are very few occasions when that is a wise decision. The exit strategy that I am referring to is the strategy you will use to get back the initial capital that you invested into the property. The sooner you can get your initial capital out of the property two major things happen:

✓ You can use this capital again to build more assets that will further multiply your wealth

✓ Once you get your initial investment back, the returns you make on the property become infinite returns on your investment, as you no longer have any of your own money left in the deal.

5. **Find an ideal area in which to buy**

    Once you've decided on your strategy, you can then select the most appropriate area to invest in. It might be in your own neighborhood or it might be in another part of the country. It may even be in a different country altogether. Just make sure that you know the area before you invest in it. One of the biggest mistakes people make comes from chasing the next real estate "hot spot" without fully understanding the area where the property is located. The more you know about the area, the easier it will be to determine whether a property is a good deal or not.

6. **Identify/Analyse properties**

    By learning how to analyze property you will be able to tell good deals from bad deals. When buying your own home, you buy on emotion. When buying a property as an investment, you have to think with your calculator and not with your heart. By analyzing the numbers rather than your feelings, you can identify whether you have found a good deal or not. You have to consider things such as:

    - ✓ The asking price
    - ✓ The amount the seller is willing to accept
    - ✓ The rental income that the property will generate
    - ✓ The property management fees
    - ✓ The costs that will be incurred to improve the property
    - ✓ The end value once the property is improved
    - ✓ The deposit required
    - ✓ The amount you will be able to borrow on the property
    - ✓ The mortgage payment you will need to make
    - ✓ The potential growth of the property
    - ✓ The ongoing expenses of the property
    - ✓ The void periods where you may not have a tenant in the property
    - ✓ The size of the property

    Once you have evaluated all of these factors, you can begin to think about the available options for increasing the value of the property—and this is where you can get really creative. You can start to brainstorm ways to best optimize the growth potential of the property, and therefore accelerate your wealth.

7. **Negotiating the deal**

Once you have decided on your strategy, identified the area in which you want to invest, and used analysis to settle on the exact property you want, the next step is to negotiate the deal.

In effect you are now finalizing the actual purchase price of the property, and of course, you want to buy the property for the lowest price you can. However, it is more important that you and the seller both get what you want from the deal. There are many ways that you can pressure sellers into selling low, but if it isn't a *win/win* for both parties, the sellers may feel that they are not being treated with respect and dignity. I have seen many deals fall through just because the buyer was too greedy in the negotiations. The best deals are those that make both parties happy. Having said this, it is vitally important that you have in mind a maximum price that you will not go over, and be prepared walk away from the deal if the numbers just don't add up.

When negotiating a price for any property it is usually best if you can get the seller to name a price before you make an offer, as this gives you a better starting point to begin the negotiations. You then make an offer for the property, either through the real estate agent selling the property or directly with the seller. The seller will accept the offer, reject the offer, or come back with a counter offer of another price. Just remember that if the seller accepts your first offer, you will always wonder how low of a price you may have been able to get, so don't be afraid to offer a low price to start with. Once the seller comes back with a rejection of the offer or a counter offer, you can go back in with another, slightly higher offer until you both come to an agreement on the final price. If you've done your homework, you should be able to recognize the homes that are fantastic deals at the asking price. This will ensure that you don't lose out on the property by spending too much time haggling over the final price, as there may be someone else in line looking to buy the same property.

8. **Funding the deal**

   At this stage, your offer on the property has been accepted. Based on previous discussions with your mortgage broker, you already know what size mortgage you will be able to get to purchase the property. Now, it is just a matter of completing the mortgage application with your broker so that he or she can bring the mortgage and your purchasing fund together in order to close on the property.

9. **Managing the property**

   Now you need to decide how you are going to manage your property. If you plan to let the property out yourself, you'll need to do all the legwork of finding a tenant, running all the necessary checks for each applicant, signing the relevant contracts and collecting the security deposit, or bond, and rent yourself. Or, you could choose to employ a letting agent to do all of this for you.

   If you employ a letting agent, he or she will take a percentage of the monthly rent, and an initial payment for renting the property out. A letting agent will also have a stream of potential new tenants coming through her door on a regular basis, whereas you would have to go out and find a tenant yourself through advertising. The longer it takes you to find a tenant for the property, the longer you will have to finance the mortgage on your own, and this could cost you far more over the long run than paying the fees that the letting agent charges. A good letting agent will save you money and time, so I would always recommend using one.

   On this point, just two days ago I received a call from my letting agent informing me that due to personal reasons, a tenant in one of my apartments had moved out early from my property to live back home with his parents. He was half-way through his six-month tenancy, leaving me in the position of not having my property tenanted. The thought of having to go out and find a new tenant on such short notice, when I have a business to run, a book to finish writing, and family commitments, would have been a cause of major stress. But because I have a good letting agent, I was able to leave it in his hands. Normally, when a tenant is due to move out, the letting agent will begin marketing the property at least a month in advance in order to line up a new tenant as quickly as possible.

Using such a strategy shortens the gap between tenants, and minimises the length of time the owner must be solely responsible for loan costs. However, because this tenant moved out on very short notice, there had been no time to market the property, and initially I thought that I might be left with a bit of a gap. My letting agent called me the next day to say he had found a new tenant who wanted to move into the apartment the following day, was agreeable to a twelve-month contract, wanted to pay six months' rent in advance, and was now going to pay me £25 per month more rent than the previous tenant was paying. This story just goes to show why having a good letting agent in place to manage your property is well worth the investment. This is why I highly recommend finding a good agent in the area that you have chosen to purchase your investment property.

MONEY PUZZLE MASTERY EXERCISES—
BUILDING YOUR OWN ASSETS

After reading this chapter and seriously thinking about its content, what are the three most important things for you to remember about *building your own assets*?

1. _____
2. _____
3. _____

How has learning this affected the way you think about your financial future?

_____

_____

_____

_____

As a result of what you learned from this chapter, what actions do you intend to take in order to create a more successful and abundant future?

1. _____
2. _____
3. _____
4. _____
5. _____

Have you ever thought about investing in shares?

_____

_____

_____

_____

What past experiences—if any—have you had with investing in the stock market?

_____

_____

_____

_____

What do you think you would need to learn in order to become successful investing in the stock market?

_____

_____

_____

_____

Have you ever thought about starting a business?

_____

_____

_____

_____

What past experience—if any—have you had with running a business?

_____

_____

_____

_____

What do you think you would need to learn in order to become a successful business owner?

_____

_____

_____

_____

Have you ever thought about investing in property?

_____

_____

_____

_____

What past experience—if any—have you had with property ownership?

_____

_____

_____

_____

What do you think you would need to learn in order to become successful investing in property?

_____

_____

_____

_____

9

THE MULTIPLIER THAT ACCELERATES YOUR WEALTH

MORTGAGES —JUST A DEBT OR A TOOL FOR BUILDING WEALTH?

IT'S vitally important to understand what a mortgage really is, because used correctly and wisely, mortgages are a key tool that can help create and accelerate real wealth for the future.

Most people look forward to the day when they can finally purchase their first home, believing that a home is the greatest investment they could ever make. What they often don't consider, however, is that the mortgage on this home is probably the biggest debt that they will ever incur. The mortgage liability you assume the moment you purchase a home represents a huge outlay of cash that will flow out of your pockets and back to the bank for many years to come. Most people will spend the next twenty-five to thirty years repaying their mortgages until at last this debt—which has been hanging around their necks for all these years—is paid off.

It's no wonder that many people are hesitant to take on another mortgage to purchase a second property. The prospect seems risky and frightening. And yet, these same people gladly increase the size of their mortgage by borrowing against their home to pay off credit card debt or personal loans— but they still believe that borrowing for the purpose of buying additional assets is very risky!

This fear is based on a fundamental misunderstanding of how mortgages can be utilized as an investment tool to massively increase your asset base and create wealth in a very short period of time. Understanding how to use mortgages to create assets is one of the most vital pieces of financial wisdom you can ever learn.

MORTGAGES LEVERAGE YOUR MONEY TO BUY MORE

Using mortgages as an investment tool allows you to leverage your own money to massively increase your asset base—even before you take into account the rate at which your property will appreciate over time. A mortgage is an investment tool unlike any other: You use someone else's money to buy an asset, and then get somebody else to pay it back for you.

An added benefit of using mortgages to build wealth is that as your equity grows in one asset, you can then use this equity to buy more assets. So, rather than going with the crowd and using equity to pay off spending debt such as credit cards and personal loans, you can use this equity far more intelligently to buy further assets.

When the value of these assets appreciates in the future, you can multiply the leverage even further to buy more. This cycle continues in an upward trend that builds greater levels of wealth and financial independence. Using other people's money is the strategy of the wealthy. They understand that doing so will multiply their own money, enabling them to get further more quickly.

Let's say you had $150,000 to invest in a piece of property. A person who believes borrowing is inherently risky and doesn't understand what a powerful tool a mortgage can be, might use their $150,000 to buy a property outright. They would feel safe and secure in the knowledge that they had not borrowed any money to fund the purchase of their investment. However, a person who understands how great an investment tool a mortgage can be would know that by combining their $150,000 with other people's money, they could purchase approximately 1 *million* dollars worth of property.

Let's look at two scenarios, assuming the same 10percent increase in property value over time.

Person A, who thinks mortgage debt is risky, would see a $15,000 return on his $150,000 investment. Person B, however, would earn $100,000 on the same investment by using other people's money to increase his buying power, and therefore his returns. In fact, if you look at this one example in terms of Return on Investment, you will see that Person A made a 10 percent return on his money, but Person B made a 66percent return from the very same capital.

"Ah but!" I can hear you say. Person B borrowed $850,000, so in addition to getting a $100,000 return on his investment, he also had all the payments to make on the mortgages. Well, this is where using other people's money comes into play again. If the properties were purchased correctly, they would be rented out, and the rent coming in from the tenants would more than cover the mortgage payments. So, not only has Person B used other people's money to increase his profit by $85,000, a 566 percent increase, but he is also using other people's money to pay for it in the process!

Assuming that Person A rented his property out, he, too, would have rental income, so this difference can be slightly adjusted, because he would have no mortgage payments to make. However, if the rent on his $150,000 property was $600 per month, it would take nearly twelve years for the $85,000 difference in profit to be eroded, assuming that property prices only grew by 10 percent over the whole twelve-year period. This is highly unlikely, as the average growth on properties for each ten-year period since 1963 in the U.S. has been 92 percent, and since 1946 in the U.K. has been 140percent.

THE MISCONCEPTION OF YOUR HOME MORTGAGE

Another misconception surrounding home mortgages is that you must use a repayment mortgage over a twenty-five or thirty year period in order to have no mortgage payment by the time you retire. Paying off your mortgage by the time you retire is a great goal to have, but doing it through a twenty-five-year repayment mortgage is the worst possible way of doing so.

You can leverage your finances far better by just paying the interest on your mortgage and using the repayment portion for creating future wealth and building additional assets. This will grow your wealth far more rapidly than by using your hard-earned cash to pay the bank or building society to reduce the size of your mortgage.

For example, let's say you own a house valued in today's market at $150,000, and you have a mortgage of $100,000 on a repayment mortgage that has twenty years left to run. Assuming a 6 percent interest rate, your monthly payment will be $726.54. This is made up of $500 per month in interest, and the rest, $226.54, is your capital repayment figure. If you pay off your mortgage according to this plan, you are guaranteed to have it repaid in twenty years, assuming that you have made all your payments. But that is all you are guaranteed.

Whatever appreciation in value your home has realized over this time won't make one bit of difference to your overall financial security, because even though you have no mortgage, you also have no other assets outside your own home that you can utilize to increase your standard of living. You could sell your home, but you would then have to rent, using the equity from the sale of your house to fund the rent for the rest of your life. Or you could downsize and buy a smaller home. However, because all other houses have gone up in value as well, you would see most of your equity being used to purchase this smaller home. The amount left over would unlikely increase your standard of living significantly over the time you may live in retirement.

If, however, you used this $226.54 per month that goes to capital repayment costs to borrow some of the equity out of the property, the equity that you borrow out could be used to create additional assets via the purchase of a new property. The monthly payment of $226.54 would allow you to borrow just over $45,000 at 6 percent interest.

You could buy additional property valued at just over $300,000, because as before, you can use the $45,000 as a deposit together with the leverage of a mortgage!

In other words, using the same equity that you started with, you now own two properties—an investment property and your own home. This second property would also grow in value over the next twenty years, and assuming property growth of just 5 percent per year, this second asset alone would be worth just over $800,000!

That's nearly $550,000 in additional equity from the same starting-out point of you paying $726 per month, and all you've done is leveraged where your money was being directed!

ACCELERATE YOUR WEALTH

Using mortgages—or other people's money—as a tool to invest is like an accelerator that will generate a more prosperous retirement. It allows you to buy more with your initial starting capital, accumulate more assets earlier, generate more growth, and multiply the effects that compound interest has on your money. It will also generate a far greater asset fund in retirement that you can utilize to increase your standard of living.

As we saw in the previous example, just by redirecting your monthly expense to use the equity in your own home to buy more assets is a fantastic strategy to create far more wealth than by just owning your own home and structuring your mortgage on a repayment basis over twenty-five or thirty years.

Earlier, we looked at an example of buying one property outright for $150,000 versus using this $150,000 as a deposit to purchase $1 million worth of property from the same starting capital.

What we didn't see in this earlier example was the long-term effect of using this strategy. Over twenty years, the person who used their $150,000 to buy one property outright would now be sitting on a property valued at nearly $400,000, assuming that properties had grown by just 5 percent per year.

However, the person who used the strategy of combining his $150,000 with other people's money to buy $1 million worth of property would now be sitting on a property valued at more than 2.6 million dollars, again assuming the same 5 percent return per year. Even after repaying the $850,000 owed on the mortgages, in twenty years he would still be left with a net asset value of over $1.8 million!

That's nearly 1.5 million more money—a 353 percent higher gain—from the same starting capital of $150,000.

This is why using mortgages as a tool to invest is one of the best possible strategies for creating wealth in retirement.

BORROW FOR ASSETS, NOT STUFF

The level of consumer debt in the U.K. currently exceeds $1 trillion. In the United States, it has risen to over $2.5 trillion!

The majority of this borrowing is to buy "stuff" that we think we need right now or to pay for a lifestyle that we really cannot afford to live. Borrowing to buy "stuff" that not only doesn't appreciate in value, but actually is void of value within a matter of years, has an extremely adverse effect on your overall wealth, because you are making monthly payments on something for far longer than you will even enjoy its benefits.

The biggest crucifiers of financial security are the credit cards that are pushed under people's noses day in and day out. These cards encourage us to buy now and enjoy the benefits of spending money that we don't actually have in order to satisfy the instant gratification that owning more "stuff" brings us.

The problem is that when we charge these expenditures on credit cards, it doesn't feel like we're spending real money—until several weeks later when the statement arrives on the doorstep, and we have to start paying for it. However, we don't just pay for the actual items we bought; now we are paying interest on the "stuff" we have purchased as well. And the interest rates on these types of cards are so high that we end up paying far more overall for the items purchased than they cost in the first place. Even worse, the majority of people end up paying only the minimum payment of the overall balance on these cards, because it is easier on the monthly outgoings. However, this just further compounds the effect of the interest on what we have purchased, and if we're not careful, we may end up paying for this item forever. By making only the minimum payments on credit cards, we will likely never pay off the amount we initially borrowed.

So, instead of building wealth, we end up building ever-increasing credit card debt until one day we cannot cope with the payments—even the minimum payment per month. In the meantime, we notice that the house we own has gone up in value. This is where a lot of people make a critical mistake: they decide to wipe the slate clean by re-mortgaging their home and paying off their credit card debt. The pressure's now off, the payments have been reduced to a manageable level, and all of the cards now have a zero balance. *Whew!*

The problem now is that while it appears as though all of this debt has been wiped clean, it has actually just been transferred onto your home mortgage, and you have used your own equity—the equity that could have been used to start you on the road to financial freedom—to pay off your consumer debt.

The even bigger problem long term, is that you have transferred the debt you incurred to purchase "stuff" onto a twenty, twenty-five, or thirty- year mortgage. If you work out the interest costs over the length of time you finance your home, it just may open your eyes to how insidious a waste this is of your hard -earned money.

Unfortunately, the bad news doesn't stop there. More often than not, the people who make a "clean slate" of their credit card debt by sweeping it into their home mortgage end up running up their credit cards *again*, hoping that one day their property will rise in value and save them again. It's not surprising, really, because the underlying problem was never addressed. They still feel compelled to go out and buy that new pair of shoes, the latest iPod, the sunshine holiday, and of course, the Starbucks every day. The cycle just keeps going. This, my friends, is why it's called *bad debt!*

Now, compare this with borrowing money to buy an asset that will grow in value over time, be paid for by someone else, and create a passive income for you later on in life. Yes, you will have to give up your addiction to instant gratification, but as your assets continue to grow in value, you'll soon be in a position to fund whatever lifestyle you choose to create.

So, in twenty years, when your friend down the road is still paying the interest on that pair of shoes she just had to have (and hasn't worn in years), and is working full time and more to fund a lifestyle she can't afford, you will be free to retire with the level of income you desire to pay for anything you want when you want it. This is the definition of *good debt*.

The question you must ask yourself now is: Which type debt do you want to start acquiring, *GOOD DEBT* or *BAD DEBT*?

REPAYMENT MORTGAGES—WHERE'S MY MONEY GONE?

By understanding the options that are available for repaying your mortgage, you can grow your equity fund to gain financial freedom.

As I said before, it is a great goal to have your mortgage paid off by the time you retire, but repaying your mortgage through a twenty-five or thirty year repayment mortgage isn't necessarily the best way to do it.

By spending the money you earn today on a repayment mortgage, you are using today's money to repay today's debt. As you know, the value of money decreases each year because the cost of living goes up. Just think how much a pint of beer, a pack of cigarettes, a tank of fuel, a pint of milk, or a loaf of bread cost just ten years ago. A dollar or pound today buys you far less than it did then.

This is exactly what happens with a repayment mortgage. You are using the value of your money today to repay the value of today's debt. However, if you delayed the repayment portion of your mortgage, and instead chose to invest in assets over the next twenty-five years, you could then repay the debt you owe today with tomorrow's value of money. Let's look at an example using average prices over the last twenty-five years:

For this example I will just use the U.K. statistics as I do not wish to confuse the powerful message by citing too many numbers. The same pattern would show itself with U.S. stats, as the concept is the same for both countries.

Twenty-five years ago (in 1983) the average house price in the U.K. was £26,471.

Let's say that back in 1978, you bought a house for the sum of £15,594 (the average house price in 1978) with a 90 percent mortgage of £14,034. At 6 percent interest, the interest portion of your monthly payment on a twenty-five-year repayment mortgage would have been £70.17 per month. The repayment portion of your monthly payment would have been £21 per month. Now, £21 per month doesn't seem a lot today, but back in 1978 the average wage in the

U.K .was only £79 per week. Nearly 7 percent of your income per month was going toward just the repayment part of your mortgage to guarantee that you pay it off over twenty-five years.

If you had followed this route over the last twenty-five years, you would now be living in a home worth £221,580.

But what if you had used the £21 per month back in 1983 to borrow some of the equity out of the growth that you had already realized? This £21 per month would have enabled you to borrow £4,200 at 6 percent. This would have still left you with £8,237 in equity in your own home. This £4,200, if used as a 15 percent deposit, would have bought you in 1983 an additional asset valued at £27,972 and this house today would now be worth £234,144.

You would now own two homes valued at £455,724, instead of just owning only your own home valued at £221,580. You would still have a mortgage of £18,234 on your own home, and you would also have a mortgage still outstanding on the second property of £23,776, giving you a total debt of £42,010 today. This total debt would be costing you today £210 per month at 6 percent.

Do you think that this second property would be able to be rented out at more than just £210 per month today? What are the average rents in your area for a £234,000 property? You work out the math!

Or you could just sell the £234k property, pay off the two mortgages of £42,000 and bank £192,000!

Making a massive difference like this in your future wealth is entirely possible once you understand that redirecting what you are already paying each month into a strategy to grow assets will increase your net worth and your standard of living in retirement.

This example hasn't even touched upon leveraging the equity even further during the twenty-five years in order to buy more and more assets that would just continue to add to the end net worth and standard of living!

THE MISUNDERSTANDING OF INTEREST-ONLY MORTGAGES

Back in the late eighties and early nineties, some financial advisers in the U.K., who were focused on the sales commission, perpetuated a lot of misunderstandings about interest-only mortgages through the selling of endowment policies. Many people were given somewhat exaggerated explanations that led them to believe that when their policies matured, they would not only have their mortgages paid off, but would be guaranteed a handsome lump sum of cash in their pockets.

The problem, of course, is that these policies are linked to the stock market, and while the stock market was roaring ahead, the projections of returns looked great. Anyone who had taken out endowment policies in the sixties and seventies were coming out with big lump sums of money, so past performance figures painted a very rosy picture to inexperienced investors who had no knowledge of how the stock market works.

When the stock markets started to experience periods of slower growth and large declines, the returns from these endowment policies began paying out lower sums at maturity. Many people saw that at the end of their projected periods, they were actually going to come out with insufficient funds—a shortfall—to repay their mortgages.

With an endowment policy, instead of paying the repayment portion of your mortgage, you invest in the stock market, hoping that the money will grow sufficiently to pay your mortgage off at the end of the term. Referring to the last section on repayment mortgages, this client would have been directing the £21 per month into an endowment policy that would have been designed to grow a fund of £14,034k at a 7 percent return (most insurance companies used the middle rate between 5 and 7 percent to calculate the amount). If the fund's performance grew more than 7 percent, clients would see a surplus of cash. If they grew at less than 7 percent, they would see shortfalls.

The problem was that many people were promised guaranteed returns of large cash sums after paying off their mortgages. Even if the endowment policy paid out £12,000, they were left feeling very aggrieved, because not only was there no big windfall, but now they could only pay off £12,000 of their mortgages, leaving them with a shortfall of £2,000.

This is why it is so important to understand that interest-only mortgages can be a fantastic way of financing assets that will create massive wealth for you in the future. There is no need to fear interest-only mortgages just because of the scare stories that have been passed down by people who really didn't understand how they could have used them for their greater benefit in the first place.

Interest only mortgages are only a risk to people who have no repayment strategy in place. If you have an interest-only mortgage, and use the portion that you would have used to repay the capital to purchase additional properties as assets, then it actually makes far better sense.

LAZY EQUITY – THE MORE EQUITY YOU WAKE UP THE GREATER YOUR WEALTH

Mortgaging more of your property to buy more assets will create far more long-term equity for a prosperous retirement, because the larger the asset value you own today, the greater the effect that compound growth will have. Therefore, you will own a far bigger equity fund to use in retirement to create the lifestyle you desire.

Let's say you have owned your own home for the last ten years, and the current value is $200,000. You originally bought this home for $100,000 with a $90,000 mortgage on repayment basis over twenty-five or thirty years, and over the last ten years, the balance on your mortgage has been paid down to $70,000.

You now own $130,000 of equity in your home. This is great, and at this rate, you will own your own home outright in fifteen years. The problem is that all of this equity is what I call *Lazy Equity*, because it is doing nothing at all for your future wealth or financial security. As we discussed earlier, it doesn't really matter how much your own home is worth, unless you can use this equity in retirement to create a massive increase in your standard of living.

Let's say you decide to use some of your equity to purchase additional assets. You could decide to just take it very cautiously and release $15,000 to start with. This $15,000 could then be transferred to a property valued at $100,000 today. In twenty years, this combined asset would then be worth $265,000, assuming a 5 percent average growth in property values. Paying off your original mortgage of $70,000, the release of $15,000, and the mortgage for the new property of $85,000, this would create an equity fund of just over $95,000 that you could use to increase your standard of living in retirement. Not bad!

However, instead of releasing only 15k equity, you could have increased the amount of equity you leveraged to 110k instead of only 15k. This 110k equity would now allow you to buy more than 730k worth of additional property assets, because you could leverage the 110k as deposits with 85% mortgages (622k). At the same 5% growth estimate per year, these properties would now be worth close to $2 MILLION in 20 years time instead of the 265k before.

After paying off your original mortgage of $70,000, the release of $110,000 and the $622,000 mortgages for the new properties you would now have grown an equity fund (outside your own home) of more than $1.1 *million* that you could use to increase your standard of living in retirement.

All this extra money to make your life better from the *Lazy Equity* that was sitting in your home to begin with!

HOW DO YOU FIND THE RIGHT MORTGAGE?

Using a quality mortgage broker is vital. It's worth taking the time to make sure you find one who understands your particular circumstances and the type of properties in which you intend to invest.

An experienced mortgage broker can advise you as to how best to leverage your money to meet your goals and free your time to take advantage of other great opportunities that can help your money grow.

With a quality mortgage broker on your team, you will save yourself the time and headache of having to scour the market, meet with bank after bank, and process numerous mortgage applications. Dealing with mortgage advisers who have little or no knowledge or experience of investment mortgages is not advisable, as they may not understand the market enough to find the right mortgage for you.

When looking for a mortgage broker, you should really look for a company that has a passion for property investing. Finding a company that understands financing and creative leveraging techniques will make a massive difference in your future financial security.

KEY THINGS TO CONSIDER WHEN CHOOSING THE RIGHT MORTGAGE

Whether you are shopping for your own property or an investment property, it's important to consider the rates and fees associated with a mortgage.

Lenders are always looking to make money on what they lend, and sometimes they will offer a fantastically low rate of interest, which may grab your attention. However, the arrangement fee they will charge you for this low interest rate could be extortionately high and could end up costing you more than another product with a higher rate. Similarly, lenders sometimes offer products claiming low or no fees, which may also look appealing. Usually, however, the interest rates are so much higher that you would end up paying a lot more per month over the whole term of the mortgage—costing you far more in the long run.

To find out which mortgage is the best for you, weigh up both the fees and the interest rates, and then work out how much the deal will cost you over the whole loan period. A really good mortgage broker will compare low rates with high fees against low fees and high rates to work out the cheapest option for the period of time you want the deal.

When weighing the cost of each deal, consider the valuation and legal fees. Some products ask you to pay for these, while others are free. These fees can add quite a bit to the overall cost of the deal, so they should always be taken into account when shopping for the best prices.

The cheapest option may not always be the most suitable for you. The mortgage product you choose will have to suit your personal circumstances and combine your goals with the particular property asset in which you are investing.

For example, you may buy a property with the idea that you'll sell it for profit twelve months down the line. In this instance, the cheapest mortgage, in terms of monthly payment, might have a really low interest rate with low fees for a three- or five-year period. However, this product would also tie you in for this three- or five-year period, and if you were to sell the property at your intended twelve months, you could end up paying an early repayment fee, which could cost you more in the long run. You would be far better off in this instance paying a higher rate of interest with an arrangement fee, but with no early repayment charges.

A good mortgage broker has access to thousands of mortgage products and will be able to guide you effectively so that you maximize your returns and increase your wealth.

INVESTMENT V RESIDENTIAL MORTGAGES

Different rules and criteria apply for investment and residential mortgages, so it's important to understand the difference between the two.

Most people assume that if they already have a mortgage on their own home, they will not be able to qualify for a second, as they do not have enough income. They probably came to this conclusion based on the amount they were told they could borrow to purchase the home they are now living in. Believing that they have already used all of their "allowance" of income, they think they cannot possibly get another mortgage. Think again.

When looking to take out a mortgage for an investment property, the major factor that lenders look at is not your personal income, but the income potential of the property that you are purchasing. Yes, in most cases you will be expected to have some income yourself, but the amount you can borrow is not linked to your personal income.

When looking for a mortgage for an investment property, it's more important to identify the amount of money the property will generate in rental income, the interest rate you will pay on the mortgage, and the amount you need to borrow against the value of the property.

As long as you make the math work with these numbers, there are no limits on the number of investment properties you can buy. Contrary to popular belief, your own personal income is not the driver of how much you can borrow.

PROPERTY INCOME VS. MORTGAGE PAYMENT—
THE LONG-TERM PASSIVE INCOME BUILDER

The income generated by the property over the long term will create passive income, as well as equity growth, in the future.

The rent you can charge for your property will increase over time to keep pace with increases in the cost of living, and the increased demand for rental properties. As a result, the gap between the rent you receive as income and the mortgage payment you need to make each month grows and creates more passive income for you.

This increasing passive income is just as important as the equity you build up, because it is the income that you receive, without having to go to work for it, that helps you create true financial freedom, and can enable you to be financially independent in retirement.

Let's say you bought a rental property today for $150,000, and you take out an 85 percent mortgage to fund the purchase, putting $22,500 as a deposit. If the interest rate on the mortgage was 6 percent, you would pay $637.50 per month on the mortgage. Let's say that you could currently rent the property for $650 per month. You would be generating only $12.50 per month in passive income today.

However, if we look twenty-five years into the future, assuming that the rent increases over time by an average of 5 percent per year, the rent would now be $2,201 per month. Even though the rent has increased over time, the mortgage payment would stay around the same level. Mortgage rates do fluctuate, but they don't actually rise with the cost of living, meaning your payment will remain relatively stable over the long term. So, in twenty-five years, it is likely that you would still only be paying around the $637.50 that you are now, but your passive income from this one rental property would generate $1,563.50 per month.

The increasing income levels from the properties you purchase can also help to fund the borrowing of more equity that will then build more passive income and more equity in the future.

For example, let's say that five years down the line the property above has grown to $191,000. This is assuming a 5 percent average increase. Let us again assume the rent has also grown by an average of 5 percent per year. In five years, you should be receiving $829 per month in rent. You now have an income of $191.50 over and above the mortgage payment of $637.50.

Now, this $191.50 could be used at this time to borrow more from the equity that has grown in the property. You could now borrow up to 85 percent of the now property value of $191,000, which would be just over $162,000, and then after paying off the original mortgage of $127,000 this would leave you with nearly $35,000 cash that you could use to purchase an additional property.

The $162,000 mortgage would cost you $811.75 per month at a 6 percent interest rate, and you would be receiving $829 per month in rent, again assuming that rents had risen by 5 percent per year.

You could use this $35,000 cash that you have raised from the refinancing, together with the leverage of mortgage finance, and now buy more property worth $232,000. You would now own two properties instead of one, and the income from both these properties would go on to grow over time and further enhance the passive income you will receive in the future.

You would now have two properties growing in value for you, and a massive difference in the equity that you will have built up over time. As the value of both of the rental incomes and property values grow, you could repeat the process, using the increasing income to borrow from the increased equity to build more and more assets. This is where, as we saw earlier, leveraging your money and equity will create true wealth in retirement.

CREATE YOUR OWN EQUITY

As we discussed earlier, mortgages are not just a debt that we take on to buy a property. A mortgage is a key tool that can leverage your own money to help you buy assets far greater in value than you could buy with the initial capital that you have. There are several types of mortgage finance tools that can be used to even further leverage your own money and create equity that can be put toward building even greater assets.

For example, there are mortgages that can help you buy a plot of land to build your own house. They usually require only a 5 percent deposit, meaning that 95 percent of the purchase of the land is leveraged. You can also fund the costs of constructing the property. The end value, in the majority of cases, can end up being substantially more than what you have borrowed to fund the purchase and the building. In addition, it's possible to do all this without having to move out of your own home while building the new one. Once the property is finished, you can restructure the financing to pull out the equity in this property, and use it again to create additional assets that will grow for your future financial security in retirement.

You can also use this type of mortgage for a renovation or refurbishment project on a house that needs a lot of work or that could be extended to create value.

FINDING THE DEPOSIT YOU NEED TO START CREATING WEALTH WITH PROPERTY

Knowing how you can finance the deposit you need to buy a property is the key that unlocks a prosperous property portfolio. Most people think that unless they have the cash in the bank, they cannot even start to build assets.

If you haven't got the cash sitting in the bank, one of the first places to look is your own home, as the majority of people are literally living in their "route to financial freedom."

For a very large number of people, there is a fantastic opportunity to use their own equity as a catalyst for creating wealth in the future. The problem is that the majority of people don't even realize that this option is available.

Even if you don't have equity in any property at the moment, there are also other routes of financing the deposit required to purchase property, ranging from gifted deposits from the person selling the property, using credit cards, or borrowing money from friends and family.

The main focus should be to first locate a good deal and the investment property you want, and then look at all the strategies for funding it. If the deal is good and the numbers add up, the money will always come. Too many people sit and think that just because the funds are not there right at this minute, they shouldn't be out looking for deals. This is backward thinking. The longer you focus on not having enough money to invest, the greater the likelihood that you will continue to not have enough money to invest.

I had a client recently who was looking to finance some improvements to his home. He is thirty-eight years old, works forty to fifty hours per week, earns £15,000 per year, and has no retirement plan. I suggested to him that there may be a way for him to really make a difference to his long term financial security by using some of the equity he had built up in his own home, which totalled around £90,000.

His words to me were, "I have sat here for years watching property programs on the television and have always wondered how these people did it."

He is now undertaking his first project in property, which is projected to earn him £45,000 in equity (three times the amount he earns in a full year, working forty to fifty hours per week!) in three to four months. Not only that, but he will then be able to refinance this property to release the money he invested from his own equity and use this money to do it again and again and again. His retirement (remember he had no pension) is now looking a lot more hopeful than it did before he knew how property investment can be utilized to build future financial security.

MONEY PUZZLE MASTERY EXERCISES—THE MULTIPLIER THAT ACCELARATES YOUR WEALTH

After reading this chapter and seriously thinking about its content, what are the three most important things that you learned about *financial leverage?*

1. _____
2. _____
3. _____

How has learning this affected the way you think about your financial future?

_____
_____
_____
_____

As a result of what you have learned in this chapter, what actions do you intend to take in order to create a more successful and abundant future?

1. _____
2. _____
3. _____
4. _____
5. _____

What are your thoughts and feelings with regard to mortgages?

_____
_____
_____
_____

Do you have a mortgage?   YES/NO

_____

_____

_____

_____

What type of mortgage is it?   REPAYMENT/
                                    INTEREST ONLY/
                                    COMBINATION OF BOTH

How much equity do you own in your property?

When was the last time you reviewed your mortgage?   Date:

When did you first buy a house?   Date:

How much was it worth when you bought it?

What is that house worth today?

What would your net worth be today, had you kept
that house, or if you had bought just one more
property back then?

10

DECISION

> *"It is in your moments of decision that your destiny is shaped"*
>
> —*Anthony Robbins*

MAKE THE DECISION TO BE
RESPONSIBLE FOR YOUR OWN LIFE

WE now understand that it's no longer reasonable to expect the government to support us financially, and neither can we rely on our companies to provide us with our retirement income for life. Taking 100 percent responsibility for your own life and deciding to create your own financial security is the only way to ensure your future security. It is your life, and your life only, so—as the saying goes—the buck stops with you!

You could spend your golden years reflecting with regret on all of the missed opportunities to build wealth, or you can make the decision to start now and ensure a more promising future. It's your decision to make.

Don't get to retirement and look back at what might have been. Make a decision today to take control of your financial planning. Take the time and effort to accurately assess where you are heading, what you want, and what options are currently available for you to create a truly fantastic retirement.

Please don't get caught in the trap of thinking that someone else is responsible for generating the happiness and success that you desire.

The truth is, there is only one person in the whole world that is responsible for the success or failure that you create in your life. That one person is *you*! It's your life, and therefore your responsibility!

Think of all the time and energy we squander blaming someone or something else for the condition of our lives. We blame our parents, the government, the economy, the weather, our education levels, our colleagues, our bosses, the companies we work for, and even our horoscopes. We try to place blame on everyone and everything without looking at where the real issues lie—with *ourselves*. We are responsible for ourselves, and nobody else can take responsibility for us!

You have to take responsibility for your life. You can only change yourself and the way you think, act, and feel. To be the financial success you want to be, you will have to give up all of your excuses and all of your victim stories.

It is time to put the past away and make the choice—because it is a choice— to take 100 percent responsibility for your life. This one decision will open up the array of possibilities that exist in a world of unlimited opportunities.

Take responsibility for your own retirement planning rather than leaving it up to the financial institutions that really do not have the same concern for your life as you do. You will get to the end of your working life in a much better financial position and be able to live out your "golden years" in comfort, style, and dignity, instead of worry and potential poverty.

NOT DECIDING TO TAKE ACTION NOW IS A HUGE RISK TO YOUR FINANCIAL WELL-BEING

> *"The possibilities are numerous once we decide to act and not react"*
> —George Bernard Shaw

Most people think that making decisions is hard, especially financial decisions, so they end up burying their heads in the sand, hoping someone else will make their decisions for them. The thing to realize is that by not making decisions, we are really making decisions anyway. We are really deciding that we will continue to do what we have done up until now.

So, it's not really making the decision that is hard but making a decision to change that requires effort. The reason most people think it's hard to change their approach to financial planning comes down to lack of knowledge and education regarding money. I believe that if more of us realized the true state of affairs when it comes to the condition of our finances and our retirement, it would become much easier for us to decide to change our approaches to our financial planning.

We can only realize the truth of our financial affairs if we make a decision to give ourselves the time to sit down and analyze where we are currently, and what we really want from our lives.

Procrastination is one of the most common ways of avoiding pain. But, do we really avoid pain by procrastinating over our financial planning? No. It may seem that we are avoiding pain in the short term, but the longer term pain of not creating enough money to survive in retirement could be a pain that weighs far more than the pain of addressing our financial well-being today and taking the time to learn the strategies that will make a real difference to our lives. With regard to creating a better financial future for yourself, I invite you to answer these six questions right now:

1. Why haven't I taken action before now?
2. What pain have I linked in the past to taking action?
3. What pleasure have I had in the past from not addressing my finances more fully?
4. What will it cost me in the long run if I don't change now?
5. How do I feel about what *not acting* will cost me in my life?
6. What pleasure could I receive by committing to take action now?

It's decision time— and not only that—it's *your* decision!

WE ARE ALWAYS DECIDING

The quality of the choices we make is a direct result of the quality of the questions we ask ourselves on a daily basis.

When it comes to planning a more secure financial future, what kind of questions have you been asking yourself? Are they empowering questions that help you change your life for the better? Or are they disempowering questions that keep you firmly rooted in the same financial experience you have had up until now? This is the time to be *honest*. Reality may be hard to accept sometimes, but when it comes to securing your retirement, denial is downright dangerous.

If failure or rejection were not a possibility for you, then what questions would you ask yourself right now about your financial future?

THE "WHAT IF I MAKE THE WRONG DECISION?" SYNDROME

Fear of making a wrong decision can stop us dead in our tracks, prevent us from taking positive steps for our future, and keep us stuck in a mental loop where we worry obsessively about everything that could go wrong.

To continue asking yourself, "What if I make the wrong decision?" guarantees that you will remain focused on what could go wrong rather than what could go right.

For many, the first step on the road to greater financial freedom is deciding to start asking some better questions. Instead of asking, "What if I make the wrong decision?" you asked, "What can I learn from this decision that will help me to adapt and become even better in my life?" you can break free from the endless loop of indecision, and gain the confidence to act, learn, and evolve your strategies. Asking more powerful questions won't just improve your financial situation, it will support you in realizing your goals in every aspect of your life.

The lyrics from the song, "Should I Stay or Should I Go," which was made popular back in the 80s by a band called *The Clash*, perfectly describe the pitfalls of allowing indecision to paralyze our forward motion: "Should I stay or should I go now? If I go there will be trouble. And if I stay it will be double." I couldn't have said it better myself!

JUST DO IT

> *"The secret of getting ahead is getting started. The secret of getting started is breaking your complex overwhelming tasks into small manageable tasks, and then starting on the first one"*
>
> *—Mark Twain*

"Just Do It" is more than an advertising catch-phrase. It's one of the most empowering decisions you can make. Until we do something—anything—we can never improve. Just think about when you learned to ride a bike. You could have sat and thought about doing it; you could have watched other people do it; or you could have read endless books on how to do it. And while all of these actions would give you a conceptual understanding of how to ride a bike, none of them can replace the knowledge and understanding you gained by actually doing it.

By getting on the bike that first time and falling off, we actually learned how to balance, how to pedal, and how to hold the handle bars. We learned what not to do, as well as what to do next time to be more successful. It may have taken several— if not dozens—of attempts to perfect all of the skills necessary to ride the bike, and even when we mastered the skills, there was no guarantee that we wouldn't fall off again. But once mastered and learned, we gain actual experience and not just a conceptual experience of riding a bike. And that experience remains with us forever. You could go years without riding a bike, but put a bike in front of you, and all of the knowledge stored in your body and mind will come flooding back. Once you have learned how to ride confidently, you can then go on to master the skill. You can learn to do wheelies, ride no-handed, jump off ramps, ride down steps and do tricks on the bike that would never have been possible if you hadn't taken the first step and learned the basic principles.

When it comes to financial planning and investing, too many people get caught in the trap of thinking they need to know it all before they take that all-important first step—and consequently, they never get started. They read all of the books telling them how to invest, and even worse, they read the newspapers, which warn them that investing is risky. They might listen to others' experiences and opinions about money, property, shares, and the economy. And they may sit and contemplate becoming an investor and taking control over their own financial destiny—one day.

But like riding a bike, all of this deliberation will do absolutely nothing to improve your financial situation until you commit to taking action. You can then learn from the action and adapt yourself until you are as proficient in investing as you are in riding that bike.

Getting into action requires a certain amount of faith, because it's impossible to anticipate every pitfall that you may encounter along the way. Imagine driving a car at night on a road without street lighting. As you set off toward your destination, you can see only as far as your headlights can reach. As you keep going, the road unfolds before you. You don't know exactly where all the turns are in the road until, as you proceed along, they become apparent. If you had decided to stop because you didn't know every single step of the way up front, you would still be sitting at your starting point, never progressing.

So, commit today to take action. It's like the slogan says, "Just do it." Start planning your future and decide what it is you want from your life. Don't get delayed by wondering endlessly what the journey may be like. Start the journey and see for yourself. You'll soon discover that you will quite easily learn, adapt, and enjoy the process of building a more secure financial future.

The former Prince of Wales, while addressing a fledgling organization at a British Industries Fair in 1927, shared a thought that has become the cornerstone philosophy of a very well-known and successful organization. He said:

"The young business and professional men in this country must get together round a table, adopt methods that have been proved in the past, adapt them to the changing needs of the times, and wherever possible improve upon them."

To this day the National Association of Round Tables motto remains the same:

"Adopt—Adapt—Improve"

(Source: Round Table, The First 25 Years, by John Creasey)

DECIDE TO DESIGN YOUR LIFE INSTEAD OF MAKING A LIVING

Most people are too busy making a living to create their lives by design. It was Einstein who said that:
"NO PROBLEM CAN BE SOLVED WITH THE SAME LEVEL OF THINKING THAT CREATED IT."

Ironically, financial pressures are the main reason that most people are too busy making a living to design a life. If your life is filled with so many financial pressures and commitments that you have no time to design a better future for yourself, then you are off course. If you are trying to solve your financial problems by using the same level of thinking that created the money problems in the first place, you are definitely off course. The real solution can only be found when you think outside the so called "box."

As you expand your financial education, you will begin to see opportunities you never knew existed. Without this education, you will be in the unfortunate position of not even knowing what you don't know. By equipping yourself with the information you need to devise a strategy, you will break free from the shackles of making a living, and begin to design a life of financial independence.

COMMITTING TO ACTION WILL PROPEL YOU TO A PROSPEROUS FUTURE

You cannot get fit by sitting on the couch watching television all day, and you cannot get fit by just reading about exercise and diet. You have to get up and exercise and eat the right foods in order to start becoming fit. Once you start exercising you become a little more fit, and the more exercise you do, the more fit you become. It's an upward cycle toward your goal of being fit and healthy, and it all started with a decision to commit to action, and to do the things that will move you in the right direction.

Bob Proctor uses a great phrase in his teachings. He says:

"DO THE THING AND YOU WILL HAVE THE ENERGY TO DO THE THING."

You cannot wait until you have the energy, the time, or all of the resources you think you may need to make a start on your dreams and goals. You have to just *do the thing*, and the energy, time, and resources will come to you.

Until you take that first step, you will not know what the next step may be. When you commit to action, the next steps appear in front of you, building momentum, and making it easier to reach your destination. Every journey, no matter how long or short, started with a single step and a first action.

If you decide to wait until all of the lights are green before leaving home in the morning to go to work, you will be stuck forever, because there will always be red lights, diversions, traffic jams, and accidents that can't be anticipated ahead of time. All you have to do is put your car in gear and deal with each stretch of road as it unfolds until you get to your journey's end. This same thought process will deliver you to a financially secure future.

So, what decision could you make today to start creating a better financial future?

When would *now* be a good time to start?

DECIDE TO BE PERSISTENT

> "Nothing in the world can take the place of persistence. Talent will not; nothing is more common than unsuccessful men with talent. Genius will not; unrewarded genius is almost a proverb. Education will not; the world is full of educated derelicts. Persistence and determination alone are omnipotent"
>
> —Calvin Coolidge

Persistence is vital to your long-term success. All successful people have made the commitment to persist until they achieve what it is they want. What might appear to some as "overnight success" is most often the result of years and years of hard work and persistence that went into making that "overnight success" a reality.

Persistence is more important than talent and skill in creating the life you desire. No one has ever achieved anything of real significance by just "being interested" in attaining their goal. You must be committed to doing whatever it takes, to make your dreams become reality. This is really important. Grasp it. Most people use obstacles as confirmation that they cannot do what they set out to do.

Those who succeed learn from obstacles and challenges while remaining persistent in their quest, and in the process of doing, they become more skilled and talented. Persistence will pay big dividends in the future.

If Thomas Edison had not persisted in his quest to create the incandescent light bulb; if he had given up on his first, second, or even 1000th attempt, we would not be sitting here right now enjoying the lighted surroundings that we take for granted today. He found the strength to persist, because he interpreted each "failure" as a learning experience that took him one step closer to his goal of success.

On a number of occasions, I have referred to the classic text, *Think and Grow Rich,* by Napoleon Hill, especially on the subject of persistence. I refer again to this wonderful book to quote how Hill conveyed the importance of persistence when it comes to fulfilling desires and becoming successful. He says:

- "Without persistence, you will be defeated, even before you start. With persistence, you will win."
- "Be persistent, no matter how slowly you may at first have to move. *With Persistence Will Come Success.*"
- "Some people who have accumulated great fortunes did so because of necessity. They developed the habit of persistence because they were so closely driven by circumstances, they had to become persistent."
- *There Is No Substitute For Persistence!* It cannot be supplanted by any other quality! Remember this in the beginning, and it will hearten you when the going may seem tough.

Persistence is the one quality that will propel you to a more prosperous future. However, you can't persist toward your goal of financial success until you have first developed a plan to get there. This book has been written with the aim of assisting you with these plans and providing you with the tools to execute them with persistence. To recap, here are the essential qualities you can cultivate to create financial freedom, or any other outcome you desire:

1. A DEFINITENESS OF PURPOSE AND DESIRE TO BECOME FINANCIALLY SUCCESSFUL—Declare that your definite purpose in life is to become financially independent. Decide what you want to create in your retirement and when you want to retire. When obstacles and challenges arise, remember your motives and the compelling reasons why you've set this goal, and persist.

2. SELF CONFIDENCE—Confidence comes from education and experience. It is your belief in your own ability to follow through with your plan to become financially independent. Self-confidence expands every time you take an action that leads you closer to achieving your goals. Therefore, taking action is essential to building self-confidence.

3. PLAN FOR SUCCESS—Plan to become an investor and to create financial independence. Build the assets that can be used to create a more prosperous financial future. Use your time effectively in order to achieve your goals

4. ACQUIRE ACCURATE KNOWLEDGE—Accurately assessing where you are and where you might be headed is essential if we are to move forward confidently. There is no benefit to avoiding the truth.

There are two final qualities that, when cultivated, will guide you toward the realization of your goals and desires:

5. WILLPOWER—Willpower is the ability to concentrate our thoughts, beliefs and actions toward the sole purpose of achieving our financial goals.

6. HABIT—Habits are the consistent choices that we make each and every day. When practiced, persistence can also become a habit. Developing positive habits now will separate you from the people who will end up financially dependent on others later in life.

"Chains of habit are too light to be felt until they are too heavy to be broken"

—Warren Buffet

I am reminded of an inspiring poem from Napoleon Hill's book, *The Law of Success*:-

The test of a man is the fight he makes,
The grit that he daily shows;
The way that he stands on his feet and takes
Fate's numerous bumps and blows,
A coward can smile when there's nought to fear,
When nothing his progress bars;
But it takes a man to stand up and cheer
While some other fellow stars.

It isn't the victory, after all,
But the fight that a brother makes;
The man who, driven against the wall,
Still stands up erect and takes
The blows of fate with his head held high:
Bleeding, and bruised, and pale,
Is the man who'll win in the by and by,
For he isn't afraid to fail.

It's the bumps you get, and the jolts you get,
And the shocks that your courage stands,
The hours of sorrow and vain regret,
The prize that escapes your hands,
That test your mettle and prove your worth;
It isn't the blows you deal,
But the blows you take on the good old earth,
That shows if your stuff is real.

THE COST OF DELAYING YOUR DECISION

"Each indecision brings its own delays, and days are lost lamenting over lost days. What you can do or think you can do, begin it. For boldness has magic, power, and genius in it"

—Johann Wolfgang von Goethe

Most of us put our financial planning and our retirement plans in the bottom drawer and out of sight, reasoning that these are issues we don't need to deal with today. Well, I have news for you: It will still be today when you retire. It will just be a future today, and one for which you are not prepared.

What has delay cost you already?

If right now, today, you made a decision to buy one investment property worth $150,000, in thirty years, this property would be worth nearly $650,000—and this is assuming a modest 5percent appreciation per year. If you delay this decision until next year, then the end result would be a property worth only $588,000 at the same end point. At this rate, therefore, every year you delay making the decision to start investing in your future could cost you over $60,000.

What are your excuses for not making the decisions necessary to create a better financial future?

If you have gathered all of the information you require, and you know what your goals are for a more secure future, what could possibly hold you back from making a decision to just go for it right now?

Ambivalence is the enemy of decision-making.

Ambivalence means "the coexistence within an individual of positive and negative feelings toward the same person, object, or action, simultaneously drawing him or her in opposite directions." What a perfect word to describe the dance that so many people do with their money! They end up going around in loops saying *do it, don't do it; call, don't call; leave, don't leave; go for it, don't go for it.*

If you take that first step and go as far as you can with your current level of knowledge and experience, when the time comes to go farther and take the next steps, you'll have already acquired the knowledge you'll need to move ahead.

Former President Ronald Regan once said:

"When I have gathered enough information to make a decision, I don't take a vote, I make a decision."

Don't let indecision cost you any more in life. Make the commitment that today you will move forward to the magnificent financial future that you desire. Take the first step!

DECIDE TO WORK YOUR PLAN

Having identified where you are and where you are headed, what you really want from your life, the strategies you can use to get there, and your personal plan for reaching your ideal life, all that's left to do to guarantee your glorious retirement is to work your plan.

There is a great saying that goes, "If you fail to plan, then you are planning to fail." This is so true in today's world, when it comes to planning our financial future and retirement.

The majority of people are just unaware of the real issues that are going to affect them in later life, and this is resulting in a serious lack of planning for retirement. As a result, the majority of people are on a plan to financial failure, in what could well be a very long "old age" after they retire. The amount of money we will need to support ourselves, through potentially a much longer "autumn" period of our lives, is going to be far higher than in previous generations. Traditional methods are just not going to work in the future.

So, if you are one of the minority of people who has accurately considered your future goals and created a road map for how you are going to achieve what you want, there is just one more question to ask when it comes to actually working your plan.

Why wouldn't you?

DECIDE ON LIFELONG LEARNING

Deciding to embrace learning as a lifelong process is a vital part of your success; otherwise you will be left thinking the same thoughts, holding the same beliefs, and doing the same actions as you were yesterday, a year ago, five years ago, or even ten years ago!

As we expand our perspectives and acquire more knowledge, we open ourselves to a host of new options that were previously unavailable to us.

I am reminded again of Eric Hoffer, who sums up perfectly the need for all of us to keep learning;

> "In times of change, the learners will inherit the earth, while the learned find themselves beautifully equipped to succeed in a world that no longer exists."

Just think of all of those learned people who were experts at using a typewriter twenty or thirty years ago. If these people did not continue to learn as the world progressed to computers and new technology, they would be experts in a world that no longer exists.

To rise above our current circumstances, as well as the limitations of our past conditioning about money, we have to commit to learning more about ourselves and our world around us. We have to learn about today's world of money and how things have changed when it comes to our retirement planning.

Committing to the process of lifelong learning sets you on a path of personal growth that will keep you ahead of the game, enabling you to create a new reality for yourself and your family.

As one learning experience leads to another, and one better action leads to another, over time we will find ourselves in a new life with new circumstances.

Remember, in five years, you will be exactly the same person you are today, except for the books you read, the courses you take, the seminars you attend, the CDs you listen to, the things you learn, and the actions you take.

With this in mind, I invite you to look at your life today, and if you are not as financially successful as you would like to be, realize that by not making a commitment to your continued education, you will be the same you, creating the same results, in five years.

It is an absolute fact that, if you are still alive, you are going to be five years older anyway. That won't change. So, the question is:

What has to change in order for you to get to a better destination in five years?

EVERYTHING STARTS WITH A DECISION

Just as a muscle becomes stronger with use, our decision-making ability grows stronger with practice. Mastering the ability to make effective decisions quickly will create far better outcomes than allowing yourself to wallow in indecision and ambivalence.

As I said earlier, making a decision is merely the act of answering a question. By asking ourselves better questions about what we can do to succeed in today's world, we will be able to make better and more informed decisions.

As we make better decisions—with our money or in any other part of our lives—we open up a new field of potential possibilities. And on the contrary, until we decide, nothing happens!!

What decision can you make today that will inspire you to start the most important journey of your life—the journey to a better financial future?

GETTING THE FACTS MAKES DECISIONS EASIER

"It is only the understanding and application of right thinking that counts"
—Bob Proctor

Getting the facts makes it far easier to know what decision to make. Facts enable us to think and make judgements, and they provide us with the truth, so we no longer need to rely on the opinions and beliefs of others.

For thousands of years, people made ships from wood because of the opinion and belief that it was the only substance that would float. They had not advanced far enough to accept the fact that steel would also float, and that steel was a far better substance for boat building in the first place. Until they learned the facts, they continued to make boats out of wood, but as soon as the facts were revealed and the truth became known, they have been building ships from better materials ever since.

And it wasn't until the early 1900s that we learned the facts and truth that have enabled air travel. Before this, our beliefs and opinions had been that birds were the only things able to fly.

Countless stories could be told of similar situations where the facts have revealed the truth of the situation, and our beliefs and attitudes have changed accordingly. New concepts such as the world not being flat, the earth revolving around the sun, radio transmissions allowing us to send messages through the ether, and the Internet are transforming the way we see the world each and every day.

As John Assaraf has said in his book *The Answer,* scientists are also discovering that most of what we have previously understood about the way our brain works is now obsolete.

As we learn more and more facts about the way we think and how the brain functions, untold benefits could arise from our better understanding.

How does all of this relate to our financial lives?

If we want to make better decisions in our lives, we need to think accurately about our situations. We cannot think accurately about our situations until we know the facts and can separate the facts from mere information, opinion, and belief. There is so much information available to us today that is not based upon facts. Unless we really analyze it, we can easily be led to believe that our situations are totally different than what they actually are. Too many people today are guided entirely by that which they hear, the whisperings of gossip and opinion, and all they read in the newspapers and hear on the television.

Once the details of our current financial situations have been revealed, we can then separate them into important and unimportant facts. Once we separate these facts, we can think clearly and accurately about how we can take better actions and make more powerful decisions for our financial futures.

Revealing the truth about our current situations makes planning for our futures and what we want to achieve much easier. We can make accurate assessments as to how to go from here to there. There is no point in saying that you want to go to London if you don't know whether you are starting from New York, Toronto, or Paris. You need to know exactly where you are, to effectively plan your journey. If you know that you are starting from New York, you can make accurate travel plans to get to London.

So, decide today to get the facts and analyze exactly where you are financially, where you are heading, and the world of opportunity available to you. Then make accurate plans for the future that will open up to you.

CONTROL YOUR OWN DESTINY

As you get into action and begin taking small steps toward greater financial stability, you will develop confidence in your own ability to control your finances, your retirement, and ultimately, your destiny.

Gaining self-confidence in your abilities is about getting rid of the fears you have and learning the skills and knowledge necessary to take the actions that will result in the experiences you need to become even more confident in your own abilities.

The only way to conquer your fears is to challenge them by taking positive action. As you learn new skills, your confidence will grow, and with it your ability to take even bolder actions in the direction of your dreams.

By proving to yourself, slowly but surely, that you have what it takes to your achieve dreams, your self-image will transform from one of doubt to one of certainty. Soon you will build an unshakable belief that you are truly unlimited in your ability to achieve anything you want in life, and that you can—and will—create a secure financial future and a more prosperous retirement.

A New Beginning

Congratulations! It takes real commitment to get this far, and I am positive that, if you have immersed yourself fully with the ideas presented in this book and have taken action with the chapter mastery questions and exercises, you have already progressed significantly towards financial security in your life. If you haven't answered all of the mastery questions in the book, now is the time to go back and do them. By adapting the information presented here to your personal circumstances, dreams and desires, you are sure to succeed on the journey to financial independence.

There is a fantastic quote from Thomas Troward's *The Creative Process in the Individual* that says:

"No writer or lecturer can convey an idea into the minds of his audience. He can only put it before them, and what they will make of it depends entirely upon themselves—assimilation is a process no one can carry out for us"

Assimilation means to absorb, incorporate, digest, integrate, and adapt. I have placed before you my ideas to help you solve your own personal money puzzle. What you make of it depends entirely on you and the actions you take to move forward intelligently toward greater financial security.

No one can grow for us; each of us must grow for ourselves. The pieces of the puzzle have been laid out before you; now you must use them to create a solid financial future.

If you haven't already, now is the time to start on your journey toward greater financial freedom.

The way you get results is by having total clarity about what you want, figuring out what's stopping you, and acquiring the skills, knowledge, and confidence to break through until you get everything you want.

There is no getting away from the fact that there are very serious trends affecting our long-term financial security.

There is no getting away from the fact that one day we will want to retire in comfort.

Only you can make the decision to create the life you truly desire. The information you have already is essential, but what you really need is total *focus* on what it is you want from your life.

My sincere hope is that this book has rekindled your inner spirit to become financially independent and secure, and to illuminate your innate and unlimited power to create anything you want from your life.

Each chapter in this book highlighted various concepts that you must begin to use if you are to enjoy the benefits of a financially successful and fulfilled life. As you have now read the entire book, I would like to recommend that you go back to the beginning and compare where you are in your thinking, awareness, results, and optimism about the future against where you were when you started this journey.

You now have all the key pieces it takes to create financial security and solve your money puzzle. Now you must use them. You can and will create a life of financial security as long as you make the right decisions, work out what it is that you really want, and stay persistent in your actions until you achieve. I know you're going to do it!

Good luck. Tell me how it goes for you!

yourmoneypuzzle@claytonjmoore.com

"A truly good book teaches me better than to read it. I must soon lay it down, and commence living on its hint. What I began by reading, I must finish by acting"

— Henry David Thoreau

MONEY PUZZLE MASTERY EXERCISES—DECISION

After reading this chapter and seriously thinking about its content, what are the three most important things for you to remember about *Decision*?

1. _____

2. _____

3. _____

How has learning this affected the way you think about your financial future?

_____

_____

_____

_____

Based on what you have learned in this chapter, what actions do you intend to take in order to create a more successful and abundant future?

1. _____
2. _____
3. _____
4. _____
5. _____

With regard to creating a more abundant financial future for yourself, answer these six questions right now:

I.   *Why haven't I taken action before now?*

_____

_____

_____

_____

II. What pain have I linked in the past to taking action?

_____

_____

_____

_____

III. What pleasure have I associated in the past from not addressing my
     finances with greater awareness?

_____

_____

_____

_____

IV. What will it cost me if I don't change now?

_____

_____

_____

_____

V. How do I feel about what this choice will cost me in my life?

_____

_____

_____

_____

VI. What pleasure could I receive by committing to take action now?

_____

_____

_____

_____

If the possibility of failure or rejection were not a possibility for you, then what questions would you ask yourself right now about your financial future?

_____

_____

_____

_____

Who is responsible for your future financial security?

_____

_____

_____

_____

What decision could you make today to start on creating a better financial future? And, when would now be a good time to start?

_____

_____

_____

_____

What has delay already cost you in your life?

_____

_____

_____

_____

What has to change for you to be in a better financial position in five years?

I PROMISE MYSELF

To be so strong that nothing can disturb my peace of mind.

To talk health, happiness, and prosperity to every person I meet.

To make all my friends feel that there is something worthwhile in them.

To look at the sunny side of everything, and make my optimism come true.

To think only of the best, to work only for the best, and to expect only the best.

To be just as enthusiastic about the success of others as I am about my own.

To forget the mistakes of the past and press on to the greater achievements of the future.

To wear a cheerful expression at all times and give a smile to every living creature I meet.

To give so much time to improving myself that I have no time to criticize others.

To be too large for worry, too noble for anger, too strong for fear, and too happy to permit the presence of trouble.

To think well of myself and proclaim this fact to the world, not in loud words, but in great deeds.

To live in the faith that the whole world is on my side, so long as I am true to the best that is in me.

Christian D. Larson

11

Recommended Resources for Further Learning

BOOKS

How To Read A Book—Mortimer Adler and Charles Van Doren

As A Man Thinketh —James Allen

Multiple Streams Of Income— Robert Allen

The Answer—John Assaraf and Murray Smith

Having It All—John Assaraf

The Passion Test—Janet and Chris Attwood

Paradigms—Joel Barker

Train Your Mind Change Your Brain—Sharon Begley

Your Invisible Power—Genevieve Behrend

The Divine Matrix—Gregg Braden

The Secret—Rhonda Byrne

The Aladdin Factor—Jack Canfield and Mark Victor Hansen

The Power Of Focus—Jack Canfield, Mark Victor Hansen, and Les Hewitt

The Success Principles—Jack Canfield

The Seven Spiritual Laws Of Success—Deepak Chopra

Power Freedom and Grace—Deepak Chopra

Influence—Robert Cialdini

The Richest Man in Babylon—George S. Clason

Acres of Diamonds—Russell Cornwell

Keys To The Vault—Keith Cunningham

Evolve Your Brain—Joe Dispenza

The Power Of Intention—Dr. Wayne Dyer

Remarkable Leadership—Kevin Eikenberry
The Four Hour Work Week—Timothy Ferris
Man's Search For Meaning—Victor Frankl
The E Myth—Michael Gerber
Purple Cow —Seth Godin
Unleashing The Ideavirus—Seth Godin
The Master Key System—Charles Haanel
The One Minute Millionaire—Mark Victor Hansen and Robert Allen
Think and Grow Rich—Napoleon Hill
The Law of Success – Napoleon Hill
Working With The Law—Raymond Holliwell
Success Intelligence—Robert Holden
The Present—Spencer Johnson
Who Moved My Cheese—Spencer Johnson
Rich Dad Poor Dad—Robert Kiyosaki
Prophecy—Robert Kiyosaki
Retire Young Retire Rich—Robert Kiyosaki
The Millionaire Maker—Loral Langemeier
The Greatest Salesman In The World—Og Mandino
Ready, Fire, Aim—Michael Masterson
Your Destiny Switch—Peggy McColl
21 Distinctions Of Wealth—Peggy McColl
The Power of Your Subconscious Mind—Joseph Murphy
Money —Arnold Patent
You can Have It All— Arnold Patent
The Power Of Positive Thinking—Norman Vincent Peale
The Road Less Travelled—M Scott Peck
Success Built To Last—Jerry Porras, Stewart Emery, and Mark Thompson
You Were Born Rich—Bob Proctor
The Science Of Success—James Arthur Ray
Harmonic Wealth—James Arthur Ray
Unlimited Power— Anthony Robbins
Awaken The Giant Within—Anthony Robbins
The Millionaire Mindset—Gerry Robert
The Seasons Of Life—Jim Rohn
Twelve Pillars —Jim Rohn and Chris Widener

Real Estate Riches—Dolf de Roos
Natural Brilliance —Paul Scheele
Happy For No Reason—Marci Shimoff
Unlimited Futures—Bobbie Stevens
The Success System That Never Fails—W. Clement Stone
How The Best Get Better—Dan Sullivan
Quantum Success—Sandra Anne Taylor
The Power Of Now—Eckhart Tolle
A New Earth—Eckhart Tolle
Flight Plan—Brian Tracy
The Edinburgh Lectures on Mental Science—Thomas Troward
Dore Lectures on Mental Science—Thomas Troward
The Creative Process In The Individual —Thomas Troward
The Soul Of Money—Lynne Twist
The Key—Joe Vitale
The Science Of Getting Rich—Wallace Wattles
The Purpose Driven Life—Wallace Wattles
The Law Of Attraction —Wallace Wattles
The Law Of Opulence— Wallace Wattles
The Angel Inside—Chris Widener
See You At The Top—Zig Ziglar

Multi-Media Programs

The Time Of Your Life—Anthony Robbins
Personal Power II—Anthony Robbins
Creating Lasting Change—Anthony Robbins
Born Rich—Bob Proctor
The Success Puzzle—Bob Proctor
The Art Of Thinking—Bob Proctor
The Science Of Getting Rich—Bob Proctor
Rich Dad's Road To Riches—Robert Kiyosaki
You Can Choose To Be Rich—Robert Kiyosaki
Teach To Be Rich—Robert Kiyosaki
Effortless Success—Jack Canfield with Paul Scheele
Breakthrough To Success—Jack Canfield
Abundance For Life—Paul Scheele

Harmonic Wealth—James Arthur Ray
Mindset For Success—John Assaraf, OneCoach
The Making Of A Leader Weekend—Jim Rohn
2004 Weekend Leadership Event—Jim Rohn
Claim Your Power Now, Volume 1—Vic Johnson
The Secret—Rhonda Byrne

ABOUT THE AUTHOR

CLAYTON Moore is an entrepreneur, investor, and financial coach. His successful career in the financial services industry started in 1995 when, at the age of twenty-one, he became one of the youngest personal financial advisors to work with a major high street bank. Clayton, who is passionate about teaching people innovative ways to leverage their money, soon realized that traditional methods of financial planning left many people at risk of running out of money in retirement. Subsequently, he opened his own business, Credence Finance, and has helped hundreds of clients gain the knowledge, confidence, and ability to plan a more financially secure future. He now runs three successful businesses and has written his first book, *Your Money Puzzle*, as a way to share his understanding of personal finance and enrich the lives of millions of people by guiding them to create their ideal lives. Outside of work, Clayton is happily married, and he and his wife have three children. He is also a talented footballer, having been capped at international level when he was just seventeen years old. He can be reached at clayton@claytonjmoore.com.